GW01086962

EDUPRENEUR

How To Monetise Your Expertise & Profitably Educate Your Market

SARAH CORDINER

A GIFT FOR MY READERS

Take Sarah's 'Create Your Course Plan 5 Day Challenge'
for FREE
Simply visit: www.sarahcordiner.com/courseplanchallenge
Join the Facebook group 'Entrepreneur to Edupreneur'

ISBN-13: 978-0-6480790-0-2
ISBN-10: 0-6480790-0-7

Author: Sarah Cordiner
Title: Edupreneur
Subtitle: How To Monetise Your Expertise & Profitably Educate Your
Market
Subjects: Business, Entrepreneurship, Marketing, Adult Education, Curriculum Design

Disclaimer: The material in this publication is of the nature of general comment only, and does not represent professional advice. It is not intended to provide specific guidance for particular circumstances, and it should not be relied upon as the basis for any decision to take action or not take action on any matter which it covers. Readers should obtain professional advice where appropriate, before making any such decision. To the maximum extent permitted by law, the author and publisher disclaim all responsibility and liability to any person, arising directly or indirectly from any person taking action or not taking action based on the information in this publication.
The moral rights of the author have been asserted.

Copyright Sarah Cordiner MainTraining 2017

Contents

Acknowledgements

This book goes out to YOU. I dedicate every lovingly written page to my fellow Edupreneurs; past, present and future.

In this book, I wish to recognise, celebrate and appraise those who are building a business around not just their own bottom line, but around contributing to the body of knowledge within their industry; around contributing to the knowledge, skills and capabilities of their marketplace.

The people who I call, Edupreneurs.

You are the people that selflessly learn, continuously develop and expand upon your own expertise – and then spend hours and hours finding ways to share that knowledge with others.

Whether it be through webinars seminars, face to face courses, online courses, how-to guides, books, eBooks, video tutorials, or the many other ways of sharing your expertise.

Whether it's for profit in its own right, or as a lead generation tool for your primary products and services.

Edupreneurs have discovered and tapped into something powerful that most entrepreneurs have not, and this sees you far ahead of your entrepreneurial competitors; especially as we enter a new era of doing business.

The world of business has changed. Our customers have changed how they want to engage with suppliers and service providers has changed.

1

Those who carry on doing business the old way – telling and selling – will die out as a new , stronger, more influential breed of entrepreneur comes forth.

The edupreneur has realised that we can no longer just go out there and sell.

They have realised that we need to attract and retain our customers buy giving them information and EDUCATION.

We have to share our best kept secrets, provide the recipes to our most special dish and freely expose our winning strategies to win customers over and create paying and raving fans. They will no longer tolerate the sales pitch.

They're hungry for information and knowledge, and by giving it to them we get to DEMONSTRATE our credibility, capability and expertise as much as they get to EXPERIENCE it.

I was once guest speaking at a high end event; some of the delegates there had paid my client more than $36,000 each to be there – so I conducted a little experiment to illustrate my point that 'education is the new business super power'.

I asked the audience how they had come to be at that high paid event by a show of hands.

I first asked them, how many were there as a result of the website that promoted the event, the perfectly designed brochures, the TV ads or the sensational lead pages all over Facebook. Not one single person raised their hand.

When I asked them how many had paid 5 figures as a result of attending a FREE preliminary training workshop, the entire room raised their hands.

Education IS the new currency, regardless of what business you're in.

Edupreneurs have realised that giving away your trade secrets WILL win you the trade. That credibility is only generated by your customer consistently experiencing your expertise, as this is the true catalyst for trust and sales.

Using the platform of education is not restricted to training providers and educators. Regardless of your industry, it gets you in front of many more people than traditional sales – increasing your exposure, leads, sales and your authority positioning – he who teaches a topic is automatically seen as the guru in it – provided you teach it well of course.

Edupreneurs have also realised that a little goes a long way.

That success does not come overnight.

That a persistent and consistent message goes a long way in creating desired results and getting business by referrals – especially when done with oodles of passion.

It was quite some time ago that I decided I wanted to be an edupreneur – to go into the business of educating others. I'll never forget having my business dream crushed by those I most loved. They told me to *'get real'*, *'get my head out of the clouds' and to 'get a proper job'. What does that even mean anyway?*

I was hurt, but I had a fire burning inside of me that urged me to do it regardless - and thank goodness that I did.

You see, edupreneurs are unique.

We are different because we are intrinsically futuristic. We can see things that haven't happened yet, so clearly that they bravely risk everything to pursue its fruition.

We are not understood by the rest of the world.

Our ideas are ridiculed and opposed until they have materialised.

We work passionately and tirelessly, often without pay, to make a new idea come to life.

We do all this not just for ourselves, but because we feel that they have something that can make the world better – and we DO.

We don't have a boss to praise us or pat us on the back when we've overcome the toughest challenges.

We don't get offered a paid day off when we are tired.

We often cannot share our victories with our friends and family for fear of looking like a bragger – despite the fact that achieving the victory may have nearly killed us.

We often cannot share our fears, failures and troubles for fear of looking like an 'ungrateful complainer' when we 'have such a PERFECT life as our own boss'.

We know that there is no magic epiphany to the perfect idea.

That there is no perfect recipe for success.

That everything we have, are and do are the results of hard work, persistence and dedication.

Of unwavering commitment in the face of adversity, of innovative resourcefulness in times of drought.

We persist because of our passion and because the world needs change creators, movement makers and efficacy effectors like us.

For this is how this book was born, and how every movement is created.

A decision, followed by deliberate action.

One step is all it takes to make our dreams come true.

You are stepping forward right now by reading this book. And so I acknowledge you and dedicate this book to you, my fellow edupreneur.

Your message, knowledge and expertise will help people in ways you cannot even imagine.

Keep sharing, keep giving, keep edupreneuring and keep changing the world – because the world will change when you do.

I hope that this book will provide you with information and strategies that will help you with your mission.

Sarah x

Preface: Dad's Right

It was February 2012, my wedding day. The sun had made a rare appearance which warmed the wintery crisp air. From the head table I looked around the silk-laden gazebo at the smiling faces of my friends and family. My dad was just getting up to present his speech about me. I nervously took a long swig on my champagne and hoped he wouldn't tell the *really* bad stories...

My lovely dad recited stories about my childhood, he had endless things to say about the mischief I'd got into, much to the delight of my friends. But by the time he worked his way up to my adulthood, it became painfully apparent that Dad had no idea what to say. As he stumbled his way awkwardly through trying to explain what I do for a living, my stomach turned inside out and a tear welled up in my eyes at the fact it was obvious that he had precisely zero idea what I did for a living. Considering by that point that I'd been running my education and curriculum design company for 6 years, it really stung that he didn't know a thing about me.

His voice drowned away behind the buzzing of my thoughts *"How could Dad not know about the biggest part of my life?"*. I swigged on my champagne again, half conscious of the guests laughing hysterically about something else my dad was saying but I couldn't hear.

I watched the bubbles ping to the surface of my glass as I placed it heavily back onto the table.

"Hang on a minute". I thought. *"This isn't poor old dad's fault at all!"* I realised. *"This is MY fault. This is the clearest possible sign ever, that my*

marketing SUCKS!. If my own Dad doesn't know what I do and how I help my customers for a living, then how on earth could I expect my customers to know?!"

The guests suddenly began cheering loudly and filled the gazebo with applause, awakening me suddenly from my enlightenment. *"Thank you Graham!"* the best man boomed, taking his role as MC a little too seriously. *"Yes, thank you Dad"* I agreed. *"You're the best".*

Dad taught me the most powerful lesson on my wedding day that has later contributed to my success enormously.

He made me realise that we can be so consumed in our business every day, that it's almost impossible for us to imagine that those around us, and our customers, are not.

We bury our heads in our business all day, we fuss over websites and social media pages, but we often forget that unless we explicitly tell people exactly HOW we can help them, then they have absolutely no chance of knowing.

Immediately after our wedding day, my husband went back to work away at sea for a few months, whilst I packed up my bags and left the UK to start a new life for us in Australia. I knew that if I was going to succeed at starting and sustaining a new business there, that my number one mission was to make sure that EVERYONE and anyone knew who I was, what I did and exactly HOW I could help them. But I didn't stop there.

I knew, that just going around yelling about that and shoving it in people's faces would not do me any favours.

We've all had people yell about their products at us, and they have never wanted me want to whip my wallet out and shower them in my hard earned cash.

I knew that if I was going to succeed, then I had to take a different tact to dominating my marketplace.

I had to SHOW them what I did and how I could help them.

I knew that breaking into a new market and screaming about my promises would earn me nothing more than the block button. I had to PROVE IT.

Enter the platform of education.

By delivering free webinars, applying to speak for free at workshops and conferences, sharing my expertise in guest blogs, speaking for free on podcasts, travelling around my state delivering free training and answering every question as fully as I could every time one was asked, I used education to *demonstrate* that I was who I said I was; that I was the expert that I promised to be and that they knew from their own firsthand experience what I did, how I helped and that I was insanely good at it.

I used this method of 'educating my market' to ensure that everyone knew who I was, that their friends knew what I could do for them, that everyone in my city knew how I could help them, then everyone in my state knew how I could help them – and then I started working on ensuring I got that same information out to the rest of the country, and then the whole world. I also gave my dad a call too!

It didn't take long to get myself some 6 figure contracts and my phone ringing off the hook with people who strangers had referred to me having seen some of my free training.

If your customers cannot see you, hear you or know how you can help them, they simply cannot buy from you, its as simple as that. In the modern day world of doing business, the platform of education is by far the greatest stage from which to ensure that your customers can see, hear and adore you for the products and services that you provide.

In this book, I will be sharing with you how any person, in any type of work, industry or business, can share their expertise and knowledge and experiences with the world to shine and help others shine too – profitably.

Here's to my dad; and to your successful education-based business.

Introduction

The online learning industry is now a multibillion-dollar industry worldwide and according to Forbes magazine, it's set to double over the coming years.

This is already an extremely lucrative market, but we are only just at the beginning of the learning revolution and there is so much more to come for those who are lucky enough to be around now as pioneers in this boom.

Education benefits everyone - the student, the communities they belong to, industries, entire economies and even the world.

Without education there would be no progression, no evolution to a greater existence; there would be no skills for jobs, no products made, no services offered and no hand moving the pen of history. But there is now an added benefit to education - one that until recently had not been available to those outside of the formal educational institution.

That is, the modern day education-based business.

Today, with the technology available and the changing way that people like to consume information – the education-based business is an opportunity that is open to anyone.

For those who desire to reach more people, gain more public exposure, build a well-respected brand, get more leads, grow a global marketplace, become a leader within their industry and create another income stream for themselves, among numerous other advantageous; using the platform of education correctly is by far the most rapid and impactful way of getting there. Imagine it - sharing what's already in your head, getting paid for it, getting recognised for it AND changing people's lives for the better at the same time?

I can tell you now, there is nothing quite like it.

I started my career in the education industry at the wise old age of 19.

Via some extremely persistent begging, a heap of elbow grease and a fortunate turn of fate, I was working as a Course Writer, Trainer and Training Manager for the UK Government, as well as running my own education company on the side, employing my University lecturer to deliver my contracts.

Over a decade on, I am a Postgraduate qualified education professional, with over 11,000 students in 143 countries currently enrolled in my online courses alone at the time of writing this.

I am the youngest university Director in Australia, and act as the Head of Campus on one of the most remote university campuses in the world.

I have won multiple awards, have my own TV Show called 'Course Creators' (available for free on an app called BRiN.ai), have 4 international number 1 best-selling books, have been listed in the top 4 e-learning blogs in the world, run my own Podcast on iTunes called 'Course Creators', and was listed as Huffington Posts *'Top 50 Must-Follow Woman Entrepreneur for 2017'* among other accolades that I still have to look twice at to believe myself.

In the years that I have been working with individuals, companies of all sizes, Governments, non-profits and educational institutions to provide workforce planning consultancy, curriculum design and development services, online course creation and setup services and endless training provisions; I have learned a thing or two about what works and what doesn't when it comes to both the educational experience, and maximising the commercial impacts on the education-based business.

As the online learning boom reached the point where it was completely un-ignorable in Australia in early 2013, the demand for knowledge in course creation went through the roof. Where we had almost entirely been delivering our course creation and curriculum development services to Government and corporates up to that point, my company, MainTraining and I suddenly experienced an ever increasing tidal wave of individuals, authors, speakers, thought leaders, freelancers, small business owners and entrepreneurs, who all realised the power of turning their knowledge, consulting, keynote presentations, books and general advice into online courses for impact and for profit. I needed to scale, and fast, as it was becoming impossible to keep up with the number of webinars, skype calls and workshops that I was having to run to keep up with my client's needs.

I quickly transformed my very formal curriculum design and development training into a digestible and practical online course that was delivered in a way that people who were not trained in any form of education could easily access, engage with and build a course from. *"How To Create Profitable Online Courses"* was born and that, along with my next 3 online courses all went straight to the best-seller spots in the online course marketplaces I originally hosted them on. Today, with well over 40 of my own online courses published and HUNDREDS made for my customers, it is still my flagship course that more than brings in a full time income and a never ending stream of customers who want to upgrade to my company 'done for you' course creation services.

What took me a week or two to develop, produce and publish a few years ago, has continued to build my brand, my reputation, my bank account and the knowledge base in my industry considerably - and in this book, I am going to share with you exactly how YOU can do all of this too.

This book includes 30 days free access to my 'Edupreneur Academy' which you can sign up to here: www.sarahcordiner.com/academy.

CHAPTER 1

Commercialise Your Expertise

There is no 'edupreneur' if you are not making money from your course, information products or education-based business.

It is critical for any business, in any industry, of any size, to not only ensure they are providing quality and transformational products or services, but to also get comfortable with being financially focused and profit driven.

In this section, we will:

- give you a reality check about making money in this industry
- shed light upon how it is entirely possible to be rich and be a good person
- identify exactly how you will make money in your business
- plan your pricing for your course, products, and programs
- suggest where you can sell your courses
- plan out your profitable edu-business model; and
- start thinking about scaling up your earning potential

Big Cash Pay Day - Or Is It?

One of the first questions many aspiring edupreneurs ask me, is 'how much money can I make from online courses, Sarah?'.

The simple answer to this is that the money you make from your online courses is directly proportionate to the amount of effort that you put in to building an audience and marketing your courses.

The second you stop putting your courses in front of the right target audience in a timely and helpful manner is the second that you will stop making sales.

The online education industry is a multi-billion dollar industry, there are millions of dollars exchanging bank accounts for online courses every minute, and if you want your bank account to be included in that, then first you need to create your course.

What you must aware of however is that these billions of dollars are absolutely NOT distributed equally.

I've heard poop-spouting marketers declaring quite absolutely on live streams that 'mathematically, most course creators make on average $84,000 each from each online course they produce'. This is the biggest load of poop ever spouted by man.

What these douche-bags are doing when they spout such ill-informed nonsense, is attempting to come up with some numbers that are convincing enough to make you give them your money, by dividing the estimated value of the industry by the estimated number of online instructors out there. Although their math is roughly in order, their facts are far off any form of reality whatsoever.

This kind of rubbish is absolutely ridiculous and exceedingly negligent and misleading information.

That is like saying that everyone in the whole world has the exact same salary because they all work 40 hours a week - which we all know is not true.

Yes, there are most certainly 7 figure online instructors out there and I personally have numerous edupreneur colleagues who are earning way above and beyond the average professional western salary with their online courses. But I also know thousands of online instructors who make very little and even more who make none.

Anyone coming into this industry, or believing the codswallop that just 'creating an online course will guarantee you a certain income' will be quickly disappointed.

Just like any business, to sell a product you have to do more than put it on your shelves. You need to go out there and persuade people to come into your shop in the first place, let alone then convince them to voluntarily give you their money for what's on them.

Don't come into this thinking that creating an online course will make you an instant millionaire - these marketers only tell you part of the story. There is a whole other business model that goes on behind an online course and a huge amount of business planning activity.

Any business that does not have a well-planned out business model will not succeed and that applies to the business of online courses too.

Unless you already have a large, well-established following who have already bought products from you that they loved, then online courses on their own are not necessarily going to make you rich as a single stream of income.

With the impacts of online course marketplaces and increasing competition out there, the price that many students are willing to pay for an online course is being forced downwards. This means that making the really big bucks in this space, depends on you either having an extremely high volume of sales - or having additional products and services on offer around them.

This is where the educator needs to fully tap into their entrepreneurial skill set and make a clear plan of how they will use their courses to develop other income streams.

Because I have a range of services, I personally now use my courses as 'bottom of funnel' offerings to attract the right prospects into my sphere of influence and to open up a product for those who wouldn't otherwise be able to afford my services one on one.

As such, I advise edupreneurs to consider that it may not be the online course that will make you wealthy, it's what the online courses lead onto that can.

We will go much more into detail as to how to plan out your edupreneurial business model and complementary income streams later in this chapter.

The key lesson here is that the more you can see your online courses as a lead generation tool that pays you, the more successful you will be in this venture.

Is Passive Really Passive?

You go to sleep, you wake up, and there is money in your bank account that wasn't there when you went to bed, and the product was delivered to the payee while you were drooling on your pillow. This is most people's dream, and many edupreneurs live this reality on a daily basis.

For me, it is still so satisfying when I see a course sale come through, that I don't think I'll ever want to turn off my PayPal and Stripe sales notifications!

I was once having dinner with my husband at a beautiful restaurant on Sydney's Darling Harbour, and I really fancied a glass of champagne. Frustratingly though, they only sold it buy the bottle and I just couldn't justify the $129 of my hard earned money that this bottle was listed at to only drink one glass. Just as the waitress came to our table to take our order, the screen on my mobile phone lit up, "PayPal: You just received $147 from xxx". Money in my pocket, for sitting there reading a menu! I looked up at her with a smile on my dial and said: *"I'll have the Moet please".*

However, there is a lot of debate around whether passive really is passive when it comes to earning money.

In short, the term 'passive income means 'earnings an individual derives from something which he or she is not materially involved.'

One argument is that if someone is putting money in my bank account for access to an online course without me or anyone I employ having to be involved in that exchange whatsoever, then it is quite, by this definition a passive exchange.

However, the flip side of the argument is that a whole heap of initial production work has to be put in to build the product in the first place.

Then add the ongoing marketing efforts that need to be executed to make the 'passive' sale - and therefore was not without any effort at all.

Sarah's HWVM Continuum

If the exchange itself is passive, note that getting the product and customer in the first place was not. I call this 'The Hard Work vs Money Continuum'.

The layman's definition of my HWVM Continuum is this:

Put some strategically allocated hard work in one part of the production line, and somewhere the process ends with income.

The more you input, the more your output.

(I told you it was layman's!)

However, the cool thing about the continuum, is that if your input goes into the generation and output of evergreen or 'long life' marketing collateral; after a while, your output can soon start to dramatically exceed your inputs.

Meaning, that if you get to a point where you have created so many blogs, books, courses, articles, podcasts and other searchable content online, then each one of those pieces of content soon begins to *work for you* over and over again in demonstrating your expertise and bringing you yet more custom, and so eventually becomes 'passive' too.

I'm still making high ticket sales from work, courses, content and marketing that I produced and published YEARS ago – long after they have earned me back their initial investment of time and effort. I am still, and will for years to come, reaping the harvests from turf I tossed and toiled and sowed a long time gone.

That is very passive in my eyes.

The way I like to describe this is that if we imagine that every single blog post we write is like one of those 'rings' of silk in a spider's web.

Those pieces of silk are not always clearly visible and on their own are not very strong and could not catch much in the way of a big fat juicy meal.

However, if we keep adding ring after ring, after ring, eventually we are going to have one heck of a web. Each ring contributes to and reinforces the last one, until we have a web that's not only strong enough to capture what we seek, but also has a vastly extensive reach too.

Every ring on the web is yet another opportunity to be found organically via search engines and keywords, and when you get to the stage where the time you invested in writing a single post has been paid for by the business it has brought in, and then each lead from there onwards found your post through an organic search, which leads them onto buying your online courses - well, I'd say that's not only 100% profit, but also 100% passive too.

If you are willing to work hard upfront, remain strategic about every piece of content you produce and stick it out for the long term game, then I believe that passive income is indeed a very true reality.

The Dead Do Nothing

Never forget however, that any prolonged amount of inactivity WILL eventually result in zero activity in the bank account too.

No business can ultimately stay alive by doing nothing. Here's why:

- The world around you will keep on changing. If you don't, you'll soon be extinct
- Eventually you'll need to update your content in order to stay relevant
- You cannot stay ahead of the competition by doing nothing
- You cannot meet the ever changing needs and demands of your customers passively

You are about to join a multi-BILLION dollar industry that is growing every single day, so when it comes to what you can earn the sky is the limit.

BUT you must do more than just build a course. You must be committed to spreading your message to the degree at which you seek a return.

You reap exactly what you sow.

How Much Money Can You Make With Online Courses?

Your earnings will be directly proportionate to:

- Whether you build a course with market demand
- Create a course that delivers absolute transformation and tangible results
- Create a community, tribe and following
- The level and consistency of marketing you conduct
- Your determination and stamina to consistently invest your time on content output over a sustained period

Those who do this the best earn millions of dollars per year - and there is nothing stopping you from aiming for the same.

There is no magical gene or granting of good luck upon the 'successful'. They simply were prepared to do what most people cannot be bothered or are not determined enough to endure in pursuit of the fruitful harvest of edupreneurial success.

You CAN make millions of dollars.

You can also make absolutely nothing.

Creating the course is only one part of much bigger plan, of lots of moving parts and of a strategy that will require nothing more than love, courage and commitment to make as big as your heart desires.

You Can Be Rich AND Good

Time to get financially focused.

'Oh no! But I'm not in it for the money'! I hear you desperately try to convince me!

Of course you're in it for the money. You picked up a book with the word 'entrepreneur' on the front of it.

If you plan on running a business that isn't about making money, may I save you some time, pain and debt by suggesting that you go straight to the dole office, or job centre right now. You're welcome.

Even charities and non-profits have to make money and be profitable in order to do their great work.

You need to as well.

There seems to be a perception in the business world at present, that suggests that being financially driven is a bad thing. It's clear that this 'stigma' has been created and fanned by the un-wealthy masses – possibly to make *themselves* feel better about not being wealthy.

Our psyches come up with endless ways to make us feel better about not having something we secretly wish we could have, but don't think is a possibility for us.

This bizarre 'poor-persons-created-stigma' against those who prioritise wealth, try to make the ambitious and already successful feel as though being focused on income and money somehow makes us a shallow or a bad person.

I often see comments in Facebook groups between people who are far from financially well off, criticizing those who are.

They mock terms such as 'six figure business', suggesting that whoever claims to have one must be a liar, a scammer or a cheat.

Some people struggle so much to make money themselves that they have created limiting beliefs so powerful that they cannot possibly believe that anyone who claims to have financial success did so without lying, or ripping someone off to get it.

This is not how the world works.

People who think like this will remain broke and bitter for the rest of their lives.

Are there rich people that rip people off? Yes of course.

Are there poor people that rip people off? Yes again.

And in fact, sue to the statistical nature of the ratio of rich to poor in the world, there are statistically more poor people on earth who rip others off, cheat, lie, steal and conduct unethical practices than rich people, by MILLIONS.

I can categorically assure you that you can be rich and still be a good person.

Millions of people every day make exceptional amounts of money honestly, fairly and decently.

And here's the thing; the very act of educating is making the world a better place.

So as long as you are providing and delivering precisely what you offered and promised to people, you can follow the principles of edupreneurship and grow a very successful and wealthy education based businesses - whilst still doing good in the world and making a positive difference.

The next fact about generating more wealth, is that the more money you make the more you can give back.

If you earn $50,000 per year and try your best every year to give 10% of what you earn to your favourite charitable cause, you are generously donating $5,000 to charity every year.

Let's imagine that you now managed to grow your business using edupreneurship to levels that were bringing you in $1million per year. If you keep donating 10% to charity you are now contributing $100,000 to a good cause.

If you are making $5million you will then be able to donate $500,000 per year to charity! Imagine that?

Getting richer means that you can give more financially, but it also means that you can give more in even bigger ways too.

Once you find yourself with profit coming in daily, and better yet you've got your business systemised, automated and with a significant degree of 'passive' income rolling in; you suddenly find yourself no longer a prisoner to it.

You no longer have to slog out 40+ hours a week or constantly be attached to your phone to 'keep an eye on things'.

This means that you're free.

You're free to help people, be generous with your time, do more free talks, serve others who are in need, volunteer, raise more funds for charities or find other ways to share your expertise to place your helping hand in front of new audiences.

Earning more means you can give more in many ways – to yourself and especially to others.

What Goes Around, Comes Around

The more you contribute back, the more money you make.

Just as the circle of bitterness and misery consumes the people who look around helplessly at the world judging everything around them; the circle of positivity and efficacious existence continues to grow, empower and propel those who focus on giving and contributing what they have to the world.

If you want to leave a legacy, make a difference to the world positively as well as be financially successful, it is absolutely critical that you become financially focused.

If you cannot comfortably think about money, deal with money and purposefully implement strategies to generate wealth without any sense of guilt around it, then you simply will never have it.

Being wealthy does not mean being a bad person; being wealthy will allow you to be your best.

"If you want to leave a legacy, make a difference to the world positively and be financially successful;

It is absolutely critical that you become financially focused"

CHAPTER 2

THE FUNNEL OF SERVICE

Having any profitable business requires strategy and planning, but having a sustainably profitable business as an edupreneur means strategising for business with our learners development at the core.

The traditional method of entrepreneurial business was to essentially go out 'hunting' for customers as if they were prey.

The old fashioned hunters of business talk about 'trip wires' and 'capturing' leads and then feeding them through a funnel which in too many cases have been designed by marketers to force, guilt trip and trick people into handing over their money.

But the edupreneur sees the process of finding and building a commercially successful business as a very different one indeed.

Edupreneurs see the funnel more as **a journey of service and giving.**

Yes, I said GIVING.

That means giving away your content freely - it's that whole 'speculate to accumulate' thing, and it seriously works.

What Is A Funnel?

But first, what is a 'funnel'?

Essentially it is a process of stages that a prospect will be taken through, by design, by a business to convert them from a prospect, into a paying customer.

What To Do:

1. Find your fish
2. Figure out the best ways to catch them (without hurting them)
3. Keep them alive, happy and thriving
4. If they swim away, tempt them back again

A 'Funnel' Is A Process Of:

1. Finding prospects
2. Engaging prospects
3. Turning prospects into followers
4. Turning followers into paying customers
5. Making paying customers repeat paying customers
6. Making repeat paying customers raving referrers

Old vs New: The Hunter and The Edupreneur

Just to make it clear how powerful this method of 'giving' is to create a very successful business, and how self-cannibalising and destructive the traditional approaches to marketing are in comparison, here is a comparison of the two approaches side-by-side, using 'fishing' as the analogy for ease of understanding:

	The Hunting Marketer's Funnel	The Nurturing Edupreneur's Funnel
1.	Hunt for fish	Discover what the fish want and need
2.	Capture the fish	Allow the fish to come to you by freely offering them what they want and need
3.	Eat the fish	Keep them alive, happy, growing and thriving so that they want to stay around you forever
4.	If any fish escape make them feel dreadful about it	If any swim away, ask them what else they seek. Then seek to provide it.
5.	When there are no fish left, go and steal someone else's fish or hunt on someone else's hunting patch	The fish now invite all of their friends to meet you too and you never have to go searching for fish again.

Thoughts:

- Imagine you are the fish - and to many people, you are their metaphorical fish - which funnel would you rather be part of?
- If you are the fisherman, which funnel would you rather be part of?

However, we have been dictated to by the hunter for so long, that this concept of giving freely terrifies most people.

You see, the hunters method depletes it's own supply, meaning that his fish are a limited resource, and therefore he knows that he will eventually run out.

This means that the hunter lives in a world of scarcity, a battle ground of 'survival of the meanest', a nasty back-stabbing existence where everyone is your enemy and giving means starving yourself to death.

It's no wonder they tell us *'never give stuff away!'*.

And so we all watch, we all listen to the big fat marketing hunter and do as we are told.

Eventually, we get tired of spending every hour of the day fishing, capturing, killing, maiming and stealing. We then give up and say *'this fishing thing isn't for me, I don't really want fish anyway'*.

Then we close up shop and walk away, leaving dreams unfulfilled and a market uneducated.

Or do we?

There is a better way, a much happier, sustainable way to build a successful business that helps everyone - the fisherman as much as the fish.

I call it *'The Edupreneur's Funnel of Service'* - and like any good funnel, it starts with giving freely.

Giving without any agenda to receive.

Give your advice freely, answer questions, share videos, create livestreams, write blogs, talk for free at events, speak on podcasts, guest blog, give free courses away, write books and eBooks - the list is endless of ways that you can give, but so are the rewards for everybody when you do.

The first thing that people think when I suggest that they should do this is *'but won't that cannibalise my own business? Surely Sarah, if I give all of my content away, then nobody will need to buy my stuff?'*

A very logical thought yes, but it's completely wrong.

Giving is receiving.

Let's look at an example that I'm sure most people could relate to - celebrity chefs.

"Give your advice freely. Answer questions, share videos, post livestreams, write blogs, talk for free at events, speak on podcasts, guest blog, give free courses away, write books and eBooks - the list is endless of ways that you can give - and so are the rewards for everybody when you do."

"Feed us, and we will grow. We will keep coming back for more; and we will tell our friends to come and try some too."

The Chef's Profitability Principle

Gordon Ramsay and Jamie Oliver, now they're doing alright for themselves aren't they?!

They've got TV shows, endless restaurants all around the world, books and a few dollars in their bank accounts. Nice.

They also have millions of adoring fans who watch and buy everything they release, even follow them around the world in the hope to meet them in person. Very nice.

Now how do you think that happened to be so?

Every single one of us can go onto Google and find their recipes *for free*, containing the exact recipe for successfully producing each of their dishes. Yet millions of us still went out and paid $30 for their cookbooks.

All of us could go onto YouTube or switch on our televisions and watch them cook the exact same recipe in *full demonstration* - not an ingredient or instruction would be missed in showing you exactly how to produce that perfect dish. Yet millions of us still flock to their restaurants and pay hundreds of dollars for their chefs to just cook it for us.

Even if we lived next door to one of those restaurants and had free meals for life, I'm very sure that there would be millions of us who would still pay hundreds, or even thousands more, to have them come into our own kitchens to make a meal with us in person.

Despite these chefs giving away **EVERYTHING for free** - quite literally their secret recipes - they have still gone on to become insanely successful and extremely well loved by millions.

In fact, the very reason why they have gone on to be successful is *because* they gave everything away freely.

If they never shared their recipes freely on TV shows, do you think anyone would know who they are? Very unlikely.

If they never gave away their step by step knowledge in low priced cookbooks, do you think millions of people would have their recipes on their shelves?

I'd say they wouldn't even have cookbooks if they hadn't have given their content away freely in the first place.

It is quite literally the fact that they gave away their knowledge and expertise freely, that they could attract a base of fans, followers (and consequently buyers) that enabled them to keep adding higher priced offerings by demand of their adoring consumers.

And that's what we as humans are - consumers.

Feed us, and we will grow. We will keep coming back for more; and we will tell our friends to come and try some too.

Just like Jamie and Gordon have done, once you have truly established trust and a solid reputation as a consistent provider of FREE expertise in your topic over a period of time that exceeds at least 12months; then you will have a demand for more.

Importantly, you will have now built such a level of trust, rapport and familiarity with your audience through the conversations your sharing has started, that you will now know precisely what they want, what they need and how they want those things served up.

This is when you can then add the commercialisation to your funnel and begin to offer them the equivalent of the cookbook, the meal out and the private cooking experience.

Remember that *'The Edupreneurs Funnel of Service'* never empties if you keep sharing.

CHAPTER 3

Inside Your Education-Based Business

As mentioned previously, there is a lot more to building a profitable education based business than simply creating some courses.

Too many edupreneurs and business owners get lured into the trap of thinking that just putting a course up on a shelf, will immediately magic them up a queue of customers.

Secondly, they fail to realise that in order to make their courses earn them money, they need to build a whole business and marketing plan around them.

Even if you are a solopreneur working freelance on your own, you still need to think like a serious, established company if you are going to get any level of success out of your course creation efforts.

In order to build a profitable business from your expertise, you need to ensure that you have multiple business elements working together strategically.

Success Means More Than Just A Course

A successful and highly profitable online course business also includes (but is not limited to) the following:

- Finance & Accounting
- Marketing (online and offline)

- Advertising
- Media & Public Relations
- Social Media
- Sales
- Services
- Operations
- Branding
- Legal and Legislative
- Customer Service
- Communications
- HR and Staff Management
- Outsourcing
- Systems & Processes
- Technology, Software and IT
- Partnerships and Joint Ventures
- Affiliates and Promoters

This list is by no means exhaustive and there are limitless combinations that vary depending on the type of business you are trying to build or grow. Nonetheless, it is critical for all Edupreneurs to understand that there is a much bigger picture to wrap our heads around if we want to be successful.

ACTIVITY: Think Like A Boss

Although going into each of the business areas listed above is beyond the scope of this book, ask yourself if you understand:

1. What each of these 'departments' would do in a large company?
2. What kind of staff they would each employ?
3. What those staff would be responsible for managing, producing and executing?

Now looking back at your own business with the 'CEO' perspective in mind, ask yourself:

1. Do you need to get external advice and guidance on any of these departments?
2. Can you do some self-study and learning on each of the departments?
3. Could you outsource some of these departments?
4. Could you get support from your peers or colleagues in business to cover some of these departments?

Regardless of your size, or how many days, weeks or years you have been doing what you do, seeing yourself as, and behaving like a 'proper' business will alter the rate and scale of your success.

CHAPTER 4

Sarah's 10 Stages To Building a Wildly Successful Education Based Business

Too many aspiring edupreneurs fail at making a profit from their courses and programs, because they were led to believe that creating a course was all that was required to 'make it' as a success.

The truth is, that the most successful edupreneurs out there have realised the online course is only one tiny element of a much bigger picture.

Real success comes not from producing a single product and hoping it sells, but by building products and services that serve you, your customers and your long term business plan as a whole.

In the past, the online course was seen as the flagship 'top of funnel' offering – the ultimate passive income earner.

But business has flipped in recent years. Now the online course has even more power. It is the doorway into our customer's' trust.

No longer is it the star on top of the Christmas tree – it is the foundation of our entire business.

By demonstrating to our audience that we are the expert that we say we are by providing them with transformational information from the outset of their engagement with us, we are able to rapidly build a relationship with our marketplace, to get them to feel like they know us and to feel like we have already been of great service to them.

If this is the result of our free, or extremely affordable online courses, then from my own experience, I can tell you that the next result is them coming to us wanting, ready and desiring to purchase our next product or service – our much more profitable one.

If you are creating courses that directly lead your customers on a journey towards your higher end offerings, you have built far more than a course. You will have built a lead generation machine that not only sells you without selling, but earns you income, credibility and praise from your customers all while it is happening.

The most successful Edupreneurs are so because, they have seen that the online course is the foundation of a much bigger plan.

There are many parts to the education business creation journey and within each major stage there are lots of sub-stages.

However, after more than a decade of running a successful education company, and consulting and educating thousands of others, I have categorised all of the critical activities into 10 major stages:

1. Design
2. Product
3. Research
4. Position
5. Strategy
6. Brand
7. Connect
8. Convert
9. Systemise
10. Scale

In this section I will explain the fundamentals of each stage and provide you with some tasks to implement as you go along.

The 10 Stages To Building An Education Based Business:

1. Design
2. Product
3. Research
4. Position
5. Strategy
6. Brand
7. Connect
8. Convert
9. Systemise
10. Scale

STAGE 1: DESIGN

We've all heard that saying that *'if you don't know where you are going, you will end up somewhere else'*.

The design stage is all about designing your dream life and planning what exactly you want your life to look, feel and be like when you have achieved your ultimate definition of 'success'.

Just as all of the best courses have clearly defined learning outcomes to guide the entire development and delivery of the training; all great business people have clearly defined 'life outcomes' to guide all of their business activity to a desired result.

This is about your vision, your big picture of the dream outcome. The freeze-framed photograph of the finished version of yourself and your business when you have 'made it'.

It is also, very importantly about what you will be doing along the way.

What kind of tasks, activities and actions you will be filling your days with and swapping every minute of your life for.

We completely have the power to 'design' any kind of life and business that we want, and getting it starts with articulating it in written form.

ACTIVITY: Design Your Life

I often play a game with my friends and clients, and I'd like to play it right now with you through the words on this page.

Let's imagine that it is exactly 5 years from now.

We meet up for dinner to catch up on everything that's happened since you read this book 5 years ago.

Put yourself firmly into 5 years from now.

We are sat at the dinner table, beaming with happiness. We are not just happy to see each other. We are happy because everything in the past 5 years went absolutely PERFECTLY. It has been a dream come true. Everything we wanted to happen, did happen.

Everything in our business and profession worked like magic and we got precisely what we desired.

Here is how our conversation now goes…. I ask you:

1. What have you been doing for the past 5 years?
2. What work are you doing?
3. Exactly what activities does that involves every day?
4. What products are you selling?
5. What services are you selling?
6. How much of each are you selling?
7. Who is doing the work?
8. How much are you personally working?
9. What kind of clients are you working with? / Who are your customers?
10. How much money did you make in profit this year?

Make sure you answer those questions as if it was 5 years from now and everything had gone great. Answer everything in the present and past tense – as if it is already happening.

After you have done that, rewind back to the present time.

Now answer these questions in writing:

1. What do you want to exchange your life for?
2. What do you want every day of your life to be like?
3. How do you want to live?
4. How much money do you want to be making each day, week, month, year?
5. What is your definition of success?

The design stage is critical, because without it you will dedicate your life - quite literally exchanging it, for activities that are never going to take you where you want to go.

This part helps you figure out what your own unique definition of success is so that you can base all of your business activity around achieving it and in doing so are always striving in the right direction.

STAGE 2: PRODUCT

The product stage is about defining the exact 'things' you will exchange for money with your customers.

This must be informed by your 'design' stage.

There is no point adding 'one on one coaching' to your services list, if doing that every day isn't part of your 'perfect life' plan.

Whatever you have put in stage one will now tell you what kinds of products and services you could offer in order to bring you the life and lifestyle that you desire.

ACTIVITY: Picking Your Products

- What will your customers exchange their money for?
- What will your 'products' be?
- Will they be digital or physical products?
- Will you provide services?
- Will your services to be one to one, or one to many?
- Will you deliver your services *with* your client or for them?
- List every income generating product, service and activity you will sell to make the 'life of design' come to fruition

Your Income Generating Edu-products and Services

There are endless types of products and services that you could add to your offerings list in this 'Product' phase.

Those that you choose must depend on:

1. Your joy and pleasure of providing that product or services
2. Your capability to create and deliver that product or service
3. Your capacity to create and deliver that product or service
4. The resources you have available

Here are a few ideas just to get your creative juices flowing:

- » Consultations

» Coaching

» Mentoring

» Webinars

» Done for you services

» 3, 6, or 12 Month programs: Online, face to face or blended

» Seminars, Conferences & Summits

» Podcasts

» Videos

» Blogs & Articles

» Keynote presentations

» Online courses

» An online academy of multiple courses on subscription

» Face to face training

» Workshops

» Merchandise

» Learning journals

» Audio books

» Apps

» Retreats

» Bootcamps

» Audio training

» eBooks

» Books

» Workbooks / Study Guides

» Maintenance services

» Presentations & Slides

» Assessments

Increasing Your Profit With Packages

After listing out every individual income generating product and service, the next step is to find ways of 'bundling' selections of these into 'packages'.

How can you combine some of your offerings into highly valuable (and therefore greater income generating) packages?

Having 2-3 package offerings can be great for giving your customers a sense of personalisation, but restricted enough so that you can systemise and automate as much of the development, onboarding and delivery as possible.

Have you listed every single way that you make money (or plan to) in the next 12months?

If not, please do that now.

When it comes to creating your offerings you want to aim for the highest level of value and profitability.

This means that you need to aim to move as much away from a literal exchange of your own time-for-money as you possibly can, and instead find ways of adding far more value than you could in person.

The Bad Way of Product Packaging:

There is a good way and a not so good way of packaging up your offerings.

Below is an example of the bad way.

I see too many coaches and consultants who think that 'packaging' their products means making an offer like:

Package 1: 1 x consult session = $150

Package 2: 3 x consult sessions = $450 (Minus a 20% discount)

Package 3: 10 x consult sessions = $1,500 (Minus a 30% discount)

All this does is make you have to work more hours, devalue your service the more it is ordered by applying a 'bulk purchase discount', as well as make your customer face an obvious objection every time.

Are you really worth less, if you work more? Of course not, so do not price like this.

The example above is essentially an hourly rate. Therefore, if your client does not make the same amount of money per hour, they see it is 'expensive' or 'a rip off', because they will immediately compare it to their own income and make judgement based on that as to whether it is a fair exchange.

Invariably, they'll decide it's not a fair exchange purely because of a halting disparity between 'what they get paid per hour' vs 'what you are charging them per hour'. This is an instantaneous way to undersell yourself, over work yourself and completely upset your potential customer all at the same time.

Don't exchange your time for money in an hourly fashion, or you'll be trapped by the hours on the clock, along with your income.

This example shows that even in the best case scenario, the highest exchange this edupreneur will get is $1,500 minus a 30% discount for 10 hours of their life.

With 2,084 working hours in the average working year, the maximum this edupreneur could ever earn by working relentlessly (literally exchanging their entire life and never having time to do anything else in their business) is $150 an hour, and $307,200 a year.

Of course, this is a figure that might be a dream come true to many – so please look at the lesson of this example, and not the figures being used in it to get the real message here.

A package that consists of an hourly rate exchange for your time, results in you receiving a capped income and living like a slave to the clock.

So what should you do instead? Read on...

A package that consists of an hourly rate exchange for your time, results in you receiving a capped income and living like a slave to the clock.

The Right Way To Design Your Packages

Successful businesses have carefully planned packages. Ones that increase the value, increase the price, remove any sight of an 'hourly rate' and simultaneously decrease the amount of work required to deliver it, thus making a happier customer and a happier bank balance.

Instead of offering your hours, you have to offer them no-brainer value.

You have to combine a number of products, services and outcomes together so that the brains of your customers can ONLY think *'Whoa! Look how much I get in exchange for that amount of money!'* Instead of *'is one hour worth that much money?'.*

Below is an example of a much better package offering than the one shown above.

I'm going to put in some pretend prices so that you can get the most benefit from this example.

First let's go back to the example we used in the 'bad package' example, and remind ourselves that a consult session in this example is $150 per hour.

Now, let's pretend that this person read this book and realised that they actually had some other products that they could combine to create some 'profitable packages'.

Here's what they could do:

Package 1: Value: $303 You pay: $247	Package 2: Value: $1,248 You pay: $997	Package 3: Value: $7,325 You pay: $1,997
☑ Online course (value $97) ☑ eBook (value $9.99) ☑ 1 hour one on one consult (value $150) ☑ Checklist (value $47)	☑ 2 x Online courses (value $197) ☑ eBook (value $9.99) ☑ 2 hour one on one consult (value $300) ☑ 2 x Checklists (value $97) ☑ Cheat sheet (value $47) ☑ We do xxx service for you (value $597)	☑ Everything in Package 1 and 2 (value $1,248) Plus ☑ Signed copy of my print book (value $30) ☑ Lifetime access to my entire online academy (value $5,000) ☑ Lifetime access to private Facebook group (value $997) ☑ A cake (value $50)

Everyone Must Be A Winner

Let's look a little deeper at what's going on here. The primary focus of this packaging methodology is to increase our income potential, increase the value and make the client feel like they are getting a massive deal while we are at it. In essence, everyone needs to be a winner.

In package 1:

- **The client is getting $303 worth of goods for only $247.**
- **You are getting $247 for just 1 hour of your time (doubling your hourly rate).**
- **This increases your gross annual income potential to $505,856**

In package 2:

- **The client is getting $1,248 worth of goods for only $997.**
- **You are getting $997 for only 2 hours of your time and a little of your team's to deliver the service (which may even be automated). You have now increased your hourly rate to $498.50 per hour.**
- **This increases your gross annual income potential to $1,020,928.**

In package 3:

- **The client is getting $7,325 worth of goods for only $1,997.**
- **You are getting $1,997 for only 2 hours of your time. You have now increased your hourly rate to $998.50 per hour.**
- **This increases your gross annual income potential to $2,044,928.**

Now how does that $307,000 look?!

Can you see how dramatically Edupreneur Product Packaging can change your entire life and business?

Of course, this is a made up example just to get the point across, but can you see how now the decision making process that your customer is going through is about comparing how much stuff they get in each package, instead of whether they think an hour is worth a certain amount of money.

When you package your Edupreneurial products, your customer's decision is no longer *'should I buy this?'*, but is instead 'which *one* should I buy?'... BIG difference...

ACTIVITY: Design Your Profitable Edupreneur Product Packages

Now go back to your list of income generating products and services and ask yourself how you could combine them together to significantly increase the value, price and profitability of your offerings.

1. Copy my table above and create 3 packages of bundled products which minimise your actual human input time as far as possible.

2. Include as many digital products as you can think of.

3. Even if you don't have these products yet – plan which ones you can easily produce and create within the next 90 days.

STAGE 3: RESEARCH

The 'Research' stage is about ensuring that you are building a business that has the highest chances of success – or the least chances of failing.

It's about making sure that you have a market, potential buyers and that there is a strong need and desire for your products and services among them.

It's about taking stock of your marketplace and getting as much quantifiable information about what is going on in your industry in terms of the products and services you have on offer.

This is the process of getting the most accurate 'lay of the land' as you possibly can to ensure that you are going to market with the right products and services.

There is no point having the best services, products and systems if absolutely nobody wants to buy what you have.

You need to position yourself into a space where:

- There is an existing market for your products and services, but yours are slightly different to what is available so that you are not directly competing
- People are talking about your topic, asking questions about it and there is a lot of global attention on the topic
- There is a 'need' as well as a 'desire' for your product or service

These are certainly not the only considerations for ensuring you have high market demand, but they are a great starting point.

The research phase is also about finding out about your competition, the average pricing, customer life cycles and purchasing cycles, what specific questions they are asking, how they want them answered and how they want their problems solved.

By conducting as much research as possible around your courses and the products and services they are part of, you will be ensuring that you are starting with a much higher chance of winning.

ACTIVITY: Market Litmus Test

1. Have you conducted any market research at all?
2. If not, you might like to read my book *'Entrepreneur to Edupreneur'* which has a whole section on *'How To Test That Your Edu-Products Have High Market Demand'*
3. Is there market demand for your proposed offerings?
4. Is the market saturated with competition?
5. How do you differ from the competition?
6. What is the standard pricing for offerings like yours out there?
7. Do customers buy those things regularly, rarely or once?
8. How do the market expected to find, buy and use that offering?
9. Are you entering an upwards, downwards or plateauing trending industry?

STAGE 4: POSITION

This is about deciding where in the market you wish to position yourself and your business.

How do you want to position yourself?

ACTIVITY: Where Will You Be?

1. Will you be high-end, or do you plan to be known as affordable?
2. Do you want to appeal to the 'mass market', or will you be exclusive and selective about your customers within a special niche?
3. Do you want to dominate your industry niche and be famous, or do you want to quietly do your work relatively unnoticed under an anonymous brand name?

The next part of the 'Position' stage, is about clearly identifying your target market, your niche and mapping a detailed customer avatar, so that you can place yourself in their line of sight, match your language to theirs and speak directly to their needs.

If this language is new to you right now, 'target market' means *'a particular group of consumers at which a product or service is aimed'*.

For example, 'This weight loss juice is aimed at women'.

Niche Your Position

A niche is the next step after you have defined your target market.

It is when you have *'products, services, or interests that appeal to a small, specialised section of the population'*.

I go a bit more into niching your course idea and your offerings in the 'market research' section of this book, but essentially having a niche is a great way to completely avoid any competition by adapting, manipulating or tweaking your offerings to suit a very specific consumer.

It allows you to go from competing in a huge market, to being able to completely dominate a subsection of it by directly talking to only a select group and ultimately standing out from the crowd with an element of difference.

Using the same weight loss juice example above, we could niche this by saying: *'This weight loss juice is aimed at new mothers'.*

We could niche that further by saying: *'This weight loss juice is for new mothers who are breastfeeding'.*

Can you see how this will now make marketing highly targeted and so will change our language, branding, approach, marketing methods, delivery methods and much more, as well as making our weight loss juice stand out from all of the other ones on the market too?

By understanding who your ideal customers are, you will begin to absolutely nail a powerful position for yourselves in your field.

Mapping out your customer avatar means finding out as much about them, in as much detail as you possibly can.

First start with general information about them, then start to dig deeper into uncovering their most typical demographic and psychographic information.

ACTIVITY: Your Avatar

Here are some questions to help you get started in finding your customer avatar:

1. What is my ideal customer's number 1 problem that I can help solve?
2. What age are they?
3. Where do they live?
4. What are their interests?
5. Where do they go before & after they look for me?

What Are Demographics and Psychographics?

Your customer demographics can include information such as:	Your customer psychographics can include information such as:
• Age	• Personality
• Gender	• Values
• Race	• Attitudes
• Location	• Interests
• Employment status	• Lifestyles
• Parental status	• Dislikes
• Relationship status	
• Health condition	

This should now have given you a great starting point for finding your overall position and 'place' in your market.

ACTIVITY: Your Target Market

1. What and/or who are your target market?
2. What is your niche position?
3. Who is your ideal customer?
4. What will your position in your market be?

STAGE 5: STRATEGY

The strategy stage of building a wildly successful education based business is about ensuring you have a clearly defined plan in place to get you to where you desire.

Success is about having a clear focus on an outcome, and defining precisely how that will be achieved. If you do not take the time to correctly plan out your business, success is highly unlikely to come.

The strategy section is about being absolutely clear on:

- objectives
- metrics
- financial targets
- product and service expenses and required profit margins
- product and service unit costs
- how many units need to be sold to meet the profit targets
- how many prospects need to be collected to convert to the desired unit sales volumes

Once you have identified these, you must then use this information to guide absolutely every activity that you do in your business.

The reason why so many businesses fail is often not through lack of effort, it's through putting their effort into the wrong things as a result of having no strategy in place.

When you have a strategy, you can ensure with complete conviction that you are only working on directly income generating or objective-achieving tasks, instead of spending every day reactively floundering from one emergency to another and ultimately getting nowhere.

By assessing your daily tasks and to-do list against the criteria of your income target and strategic objectives, you are also able to establish what things to stop doing without any feeling of fear or guilt. If it doesn't directly move you towards one of your strategic goals, stop doing it; it's as simple as that.

A plan is not about writing a to-do list. It's about defining exactly what every single day needs to look like for you in order to ensure that you get where you intend to go. If I want to make $100, I need to know precisely what I will sell, how I will sell it and how many prospects I need to 'sell' to in order to make $100 in sales.

Below is a table that I do a major annual version of every year, and also create a quarterly and monthly version of too – this has been critical to my own success.

If you are not where you want to be financially in your business, I'd bet that you haven't done something like this to help you map out your daily business routine:

ACTIVITY: Your 12 Month Profitability Plan

You are going to now complete a simple plan that has been invaluable to me in meeting my targets each year. Here is the table in blank form, later this table is shown in more detail.

This section will explain how to fill it in.

Objectives	Methods	Measurables	Tasks
Name of Product/ Service1			
Name of Product/ Service2			
Name of Product/ Service3			
Name of Product/ Service4			

 First start by writing down precisely how much money you want to make this year – this must to be an exact figure.

Write down the exact figure you'd like to earn in the next 12 months:

Your target turnover: $_____

Now you are going to create a table that will essentially draw up every product and service you will sell in order to ensure you meet that revenue target.

Your Objectives

The 'objectives' column is the first part. In this column:

1. List each of your income-generating products and services in this first column - each one to it's own row.
2. Then write down how many units of that product or service you will sell, at what unit price
3. Then tally up the expected income each will bring over the year.

Your Methods

1. In the 'Methods' column, list all of the different ways that you will collect your prospects, get in front of them, sell to them and convert them.
2. Will you offer a workshop, get on the phone and do cold calls, content marketing, a Facebook group, run paid ads, attend conferences etc?

   This is about defining precisely how you plan to start getting in front of your prospects to make those unit sales. Make sure you are explicitly clear on HOW you will get your products and offerings in front of the right volume of the right people in order to make that amount of money.

Your Measurables

The 'measurables' column will start to help you work out what each day in your business is going to look like based on your figures, and whether your goals are achievable or not.

I work out these numbers on a 260 working day year (because I like holidays) and at a 1% conversion rate from prospect to customer – mostly because it's the lowest you can go. If I am basing my figures on the worst case scenario, I know my year can only get better than that if I really push.

Eg. If I want to get 300 clients for a particular service, and I plan to get them via cold calling, then at a 1% conversion rate and 260 working days in the year, I need to cold call 30,000 prospects and be making 114 sales call per DAY in order to meet my target.

Based on the example above:

1. Would that be possible for you?
2. Would you need to hire a sales team?
3. Are you in a position to hire a sales team?
4. Do you need to consider another way of making those sales and finding those prospects?
5. Do you need to consider changing your product and service offerings in order to meet your targets?

Can you see how this part is critical to building a pathway to running a successful business? So many business owners are happy to write down their goals and a to-do list, but fail to breakdown this final section which shows us if it's even possible or not and blindly go about business just 'hoping' they find their way along an entirely undefined path.

The 12 Month Productivity Plan

Here is the table I have made which I encourage you to complete before going any further in this book:

OBJECTIVES	METHODS	MEASURABLES	TASKS
Name of Product/ Service1 How many units you will sell? At what unit price? Total income for the year?	How you will generate the leads? How you will nurture them? How you will sell to them? How you will convert them?	How many prospects you will need to sell to in order to make that many sales? I base this on 260 work days in a year At a 1% conversion rate	What do I need to do?
Name of Product/ Service2 How many units you will sell? At what unit price? Total income for the year?	How you will generate the leads? How you will nurture them? How you will sell to them? How you will convert them?	How many prospects you will need to sell to in order to make that many sales? I base this on 260 work days in a year At a 1% conversion rate	What do I need to do?

After completing this table, your final step is to go back to your original target turnover.

What has this exercise shown you?

Perhaps you were drastically underestimating your potential income and ca now see that with a little strategy, you are actually capable to earn far more than you anticipated in the first place.

For others, you may see that you have set a target that with your current products, services and resources is an impossible target and needs to be addressed.

For others, you may simply just need to tweak a few methods and products in order to get where you want to go.

Either way, a clear plan makes for a clear runway to the desired destination - never underestimate the power of this stage of building your education based business.

STAGE 6: BRAND

The branding stage of your business is about getting clear on how you want the world to see you.

When we think of the word 'brand', we often think of colours and logos.

It amazes me that usually the very first thing people do when they decide to start a business, is obsess over creating a logo! A logo!

Before they even know what they are really going to sell, and how they will operate or find customers!

I agree that a logo, colours and traditional 'branding' is very important when it comes to building a 'feeling' and a 'style' that will contribute to who we want to be seen as and known for and should never ever be overlooked.

However, a brand exceeds far beyond just what colour t-shirt you wear; and you won't have a business for very long at all if you don't focus on the most important part of branding.

It's about how you make people *feel* when they work with you.

It's about the footprint that you leave behind you and the way your existence extends far beyond your physical presence.

There is no point having a logo that suggests 'personal service' if your whole business is one giant automation in reality.

There is no point saying that you want to be known for being kind and making people feel good, if your personal behaviour online and offline is bullish and brass.

There is no point saying you want to be seen as a powerful leader, when you post content and enact behaviour that makes you look weak and submissive.

In terms of traditional brand, check whether your colours, style and shapes are in alignment with who you wish to be, but that your behaviours, language, personality, values and ethics directly align with how you wish to be seen too.

ACTIVITY: Finding Your 'You'

These questions may help you start to uncover who you are and who you wish to be seen as in business.

Grab a journal and brain storm your answers to these questions as deeply as you can:

1. Who are you?
2. Who do you wish to be seen as?
3. What kind of person do you want people to see you as?
4. What do you want to have a reputation for as a person?
5. What do you want your business to have a reputation for?
6. What do you want to be known for?
7. What kinds of things do you want people to say about you?
8. How do you want people to feel when they think of you?

Having a clear brand (your business personality, character and ethics etc) that clearly communicate who you are, means that you'll largely attract the same kind of people.

This is great for your overall happiness as well as customer satisfaction.

You do not want to attract people that have totally opposing values, behaviours and approaches to you, as this can cause disagreements, problems and frustrations to both parties.

Being on brand means that you attract people on brand, and that alone continues to build strength to who you are.

In a business that will be largely online, these 'trademarks' can also serve as great guide posts for us. There have been times where I have been tempted into a public disagreement, or wanted to publicly shame someone who wronged me, or wanted to scream out my frustrations at the world - but instead used these emotional cues as a reminder to check in with my brand and think about who I want to be seen as before I let my emotions control my actions.

Would someone who acts out of emotion be seen as a strong, thoughtful leader? No.

Would someone screaming their frustrations at the world look professional? Nope again.

Would somebody who slams others online be seen a trustworthy and safe person to work with? It would put me off for sure.

It's not always easy to be who we want to be, especially when emotions are brought into the equation, but have absolute clarity on your desired brand will help you put into place the strategies you need to get there as well as guide the way everything looks, how everything is done and who you are being when you are doing it across every element of your business - making you talk your walk.

Integrity and authenticity just mean being ourselves honestly and fairly. There isn't much more to it than that.

You don't ever have to be a different person or wear a façade in business – that is a recipe to exhaustion and exasperation.

First find out who you are, who you want to be seen as and then interweave that essence of yourself into every element of your branding and your business.

STAGE 7: CONNECT

By now, you should have:

1. Figured out where you want your business to take you
2. What products and services you will sell to get there
3. Determined the position you want to take in your marketplace
4. Researched your market to establish that there is a demand for your offerings in that space
5. Set a clear strategy based on financial targets to reach your goals
6. Specified how you want to be seen by the world as you go about doing your business.

Have you managed to reach all of these steps?

You will benefit most from this book if you complete all of the exercises in the previous stages before moving onto the next one.

The 7th stage of building your wildly successful education based business, is about getting in front of and building a relationship with your audience.

This goes beyond just finding people to sell to.

This is about building a strong and loyal fan base of followers, of people who share the same values as you and who want and need what you have to offer.

It's about opening an ongoing dialogue with them, getting to know them - and *connecting* **with them**.

The first place to start is to combine the information you gathered about your avatar in the 'Position' stage, with the strategies you started to detail in the methods section of your 'strategy' table.

When you know where your audience hang out, how they spend their time, what they read, listen to, watch, how they like to consume information - what information they are searching for, then you can shortlist some of the best ways to get in front of them to begin opening a dialogue with them, connecting with them, building a relationship with them and getting them to want to follow you for more.

Create a Marketing and Exposure Strategy

This is the stage where you would now plan out a marketing and exposure strategy for your edu-business.

First list down:

- Who are your target customers?
- What job roles do they have?
- What specific companies do they work for?
- Can you actually name some real people who are your ideal target customers?
- Create a 'hit list' of your top 50 ideal customers that you'd like to get contracts with this year

Next, you need to identify the best ways to share your expertise, help, advice and free offerings with these people so you can begin the connection process with them.

You'll be amazed at how many people you might already be connected with that would love your offerings, but just didn't know that's what you did or sold.

Start by sharing with your existing friends, colleagues and connections what you do.

Then start a connection process by simply treating others how you would like to be treated.

This could be things like commenting positively on their social media statuses, 'liking' their online activity, following their pages and profiles, sharing their offerings with your audience.

The more you engage with people online, the more you build a level of familiarity with them.

I have made lifelong friends and customers with people online that never would have happened without going to that level of 'connection'.

However, let's go much bigger picture for now. I want you to focus on some much bigger things that you can do to connect with the perfect people for you and your business.

There are truly limitless ways that you could do this, but here are some ideas to get you going:

- create a Facebook group that will attract the type of people you wish to work with
- speak on podcasts that your target audience listen to
- speak on stages at events your audience are going to
- arrange face to face meetings with your target clients
- attend conferences and network meetings that your audience are at
- run webinars that your audience would love to be on
- give away free courses that contain content your audience want
- start answering your audience's questions in social media groups
- write for your industry magazines
- go to your target audiences work or business and run a free workshop
- send your audience a letter with a gift in the post
- join a committee that runs something for your target audience
- partner with business or people that already service your target audience
- create and share as many videos as you can that have helpful tips for your audience. Video is by far one of the quickest ways to build a connection online as when people see your face and hear your voice, they can begin to identify with you at an accelerated level. Use a combination of livestreams and pre-recorded video.

It is important that you are 'on brand; throughout this communication process - which should be aligned to who you truly are, so that your personality and character can shine through and connect with others on a person-to-person level.

People only do business with people, and importantly, with people who they believe are similar to them - people who they *like*.

As much as we have always been told 'you cannot be friends with your customers' in business, I truly believe from my own experience, that being friendly with your customers is precisely how to do business, as that is where true connection comes from.

When you have connection with your audience, trust is established and a tribe forms - and when you have a tribe around you, your own strength is multiplied.

You all benefit from a sense of belonging.

From a business perspective, when you have built a tribe of people who like and trust you, everything you do becomes an instant success.

How will you build an audience and create authentic connection with them?

ACTIVITY: Your 'Connection' Action Plan

Here are 19 ways to start creating connections with your audience via an online 'presence'.

Of course this list is far from exhaustive and these only highlight a tiny angle of connection. I will assume that you will go above these 'means' and use every opportunity to build a meaningful relationship with everyone that interacts with you from the methods suggested.

I have specifically picked these 19 methods as they are ones that have worked particularly well for me in building my wonderful tribe.

You do NOT ever have to do 'everything' that you see in lists like the one below. This is simply a list of ideas and suggestions for you to pick what will work best for you. Try them out and see what happens.

1. Create your own Facebook group
2. Use an auto-posting tool such as Buffer.com to ensure that you have content going into your Facebook group every day. Auto-posting isn't always the best, but it's sure better than nothing.
3. List 50 podcasts that your audience might be listening to – then reach out to them and ask to be interviewed
4. List 10 events, workshops or network meetings that are happening near you in the next 3 months – and book to attend them all armed with business cards and a smile

5. Pick 5 customers or clients that you would LOVE to have in your local area. Book a meeting with each of them within the next 4 weeks.

6. List 3 conferences or expos that your audience might be at in the next 6 months – book the cheapest ticket to attend each one

7. Write the title of a webinar that you will run in the next 60 days

8. What mini online course could you create that you could give away as a free lead magnet?

9. Take at least 20 mins every day to answer people's questions on your topic online

10. Identity and list 10 Facebook groups that your audience are in – and join them all

11. List the top 10 questions that your audience have in your topic, and draft the short answer to all of them so that you can copy-paste when people asking them on social media, or share them as statuses

12. Turn your top 10 questions into blog articles and post them on your blog

13. List 10 online blogs or magazines that your audience are likely to be reading or subscribed to

14. Edit your blog posts into articles and email them to the magazines to publish – make sure they link back to your website or social media so that the readers can follow you

15. Outline a mini presentation that you could give at the workplace or business of your target audience

16. What gift could you send in the post to your target audience

17. Join a committee that your target audience belong to

18. Identify 5 businesses or people that already service your target audience and brainstorm 2 ways for each one that you could create a strategic alliance with. Then reach out to them with your win-win idea.

19. Turn each of your 'top 10 questions' into a livestream or pre-recorded video and add them to YouTube and social media.

STAGE 8: CONVERT

Stage 8 of building a wildly successful education based business is about turning your connections into customers; and ideally repeat customers.

This is what we mean by 'conversion'.

Converting a connection into a customer.

You want your 'conversion rate' of connections to customers to be as high as possible, which is why all of the content you put out to the world needs to be relevant to them. If they like your free stuff, then they will be very likely to want your paid content too.

Remember, don't be a horrible hunty-marketer. This isn't about forcing people down an endless rabbit warren of sales pitches or guilt-tripping people into buying from you.

It's about purposefully and strategically building a funnel of service so delightful, helpful and rewarding for your customer, that they want to buy from you to get access to the best that you have to give.

There is no 'rule' as to how you would go about converting a prospect into a customer as it is so unique to each business. Think of it in the same way that you would build a relationship with somebody for the first time to convert them from a stranger, to a friend.

You might pass in the street a few times, bump into each other at the same networking meetings, drink coffee at the same café, be in the same Facebook groups or have kids that go to the same school.

This is where the 'familiarity' stage begins.

Through these seemingly meaningless moments, you go from a complete stranger to that person, to becoming someone that they recognise. It could take once or twice to move from 'unfamiliar to familiar', it could take ten times or more, depending on how fleeting those moments are and how distracted they are when the moments happen.

Next, the interactive communication will commence.

You might say 'hello' or nod your head in adieu as you pass. You might utter a comment about the weather as you both wring out your umbrellas, wind-swept at the coffee shop counter that connects you in common ground.

Fast forward 5 of more 'hellos' and you may just find yourself beginning to have conversation. You might find out that she has two kids and a dog named Skip; that she works at the local library and has a husband who she hates in real estate. She discovers that you're an Edupreneur and intrigued by the sound of the online course you've been telling her that you're building.

Five or more conversations could pass about how annoying her husband is, and how Skip chewed up the carpet while child 1 was rubbing his own poop into the wallpaper; when she asks how your course is going; *'Oh it's live'* you tell her excitedly.

'Great!' she says, *'I was telling my friend Janet about it yesterday! Can you give me the link?'*.

And so eventually, your now familiar friend (and her friends) start to become your customers.

Notice in this example that there were multiple moments of interaction at each stage, each varying in the type of contact and content they included. The same is true for successful business conversion. One step at a time, little by little.

Don't get disappointed if you launch your online course to a complete bunch of strangers via Facebook ads and get no sales. It doesn't mean your course is bad, it means you've got a few more hello's to say first.

This conversion stage is about deciding for you, what that journey looks like.

What is your equivalent of a 'passing moment', a little nod of the head, a brief hello, a kind acknowledgment and a full blown 'deep and meaningful'?

Will these be emails, videos, courses, challenges, livestreams, something else? What order will they come in?

How can you find more opportunities to 'pass' the right people and purposefully start a conversation?

Unlike real life, you get to strategically design this process in your business and be in control of the journey and the conversation.

Each of my own 'conversion journey's' are different depending on how we said hello.

Some of my customers first meet me as the speaker at an event they are attending. In this instance they have at least got to experience me for a brief period of time and immediately move to a degree of familiarity and trust. This means that the relationship and conversion process that they would go through with me would be very different to the one I would guide somebody through if their first encounter with me was a Facebook ad.

ACTIVITY: Map Out Your Customer Journey

1. The first step is to map out your customer journey, as in, what are the steps that a customer will go through in your funnel of services?
2. Then, what will be their journey once they have purchased something from you?
3. What will that experience and step by step journey look like for them if they are moving along that pathway continuously receiving service, value and goodies?
4. Get some post-it notes and draw it up on your wall or white board

Purposefully and strategically build a funnel of service so delightful, helpful and rewarding for your customer, that they want to buy from you to get access to the best that you have to give.

Plan Your Conversion Process

Now that you have an idea of the journey, now consider all of the connecting pieces.

Below is a list of activities (in no particular order), that it will be well worth you adding to your to-do list and working on bit by bit.

Lead magnets:

Getting our potential customers contact details is considered the start of a funnel. This means offering them something that they consider valuable enough to swap their email address for. Once you have this email address, you are then able to pass them through that value of service.

- What helpful and informative content will you create to attract people into your funnel of service?

Set up your email marketing software:

This will collect the email addresses of your customers and send automated email sequences and deliver lead magnets to them, as well as sending out pre-determined campaigns or even automatic mail-outs of your most recently released blog content. There are many out there, but a personal favourite of mine right now is Active Campaign.

Set up a customer management system:

Use a CRM to record a range of information about your customers, what they consume of your content and what they buy. Again, Active Campaign is my current winner for this.

Design your email sequences:

Write up every email that you plan to send to new customers and check that they are full of giving and value, yet take them on a journey to eventually wanting to buy something from you.

Write your scripts

Write up sales scripts that you might use on consults or sales calls to customers to increase the chances of conversions.

Offer the goods

Ensure that every piece of free content you provide offers them an opportunity to purchase something from you if they wish. Make sure this is always a 'by the way you might also like this', rather than an obvious hard sell.

You can add links to your courses, books and services at the end of your courses, blog articles, in your YouTube video descriptions, in your livestreams, from stages - absolutely everything you put out there should have a subtle, but clear call to action. If people don't know that your offering is available, they simply cannot buy it from you. Do them a favor and let them know how.

Cross-promoting

List down every product and service you have (or will have) and create a map of which products and services will be promoted before and after every item on your list.

How will you convert your connections into customers?

STAGE 9: SYSTEMISE

This stage is about how you will produce and deliver your products and services - and importantly, how you will do this in a way that ensures your production is consistently on brand and providing the same customer experience all the time, every time.

Going back to your list of products, services and packages, your task now is to ask yourself *'How will this be delivered to the customer once they've bought it'?*

Systemising is about setting in place processes and procedures that ensure the same quality result is produced time and time again, with the minimum amount of effort and the maximum amount of efficiency.

Aside from providing predictable results for your customers, systemisation also produces predictable results for you. This enables you to plan almost exact production costs and turnaround times and therefore predictable profit margins.

What it also enables you to do, is create a turnstile production line that can be copy and pasted by any contractor or employee you take on so that you can later scale the business beyond just yourself, and still produce the same results and experience for your customers as to when you were doing it all yourself.

I have a process that I follow when it comes to systemising my business which I will explain each element of in this section.

I have narrowed this down into my own 10 step model.

Sarah's 10 Step Model For Systemising Your Business

To achieve our vision, goals and targets, we need systems and processes to follow.

Here is an overview of my 10 stages that I go through when building out a highly effective system:

1. Vision, Mission, Goals
2. Targets & Metrics
3. KPI's & Core Outputs

4. List of Income Generating Products & Services
5. Task Assessment
6. Organisational Chart
7. Job Descriptions
8. Automation & Outsourcing Allocation
9. Task Processes & Procedures (systems)
10. Review, Analysis, Continuous Improvement Plan

Define The Journey

Assuming that you have gone through the 8 previous stages, you should already have your major 'visions' for your business mapped out.

Before moving on, I'd now like you to think about your vision again, with particular focus on the following four elements, as this will dramatically impact the type of systems and processes you will build:

1. Financial goals
2. Lifestyle goals
3. Type and delivery of products and services you will offer
4. Staff, contractors, employees that you will hire or work with

The reason why is because there is no point detailing a process that makes you the sole marketer, customer service rep, developer, deliverer, maintenance person and finance guy, if your vision is to have 10 million customers – clearly that's going to be a struggle.

Aside from making sure that the processes you are building are congruent with enabling the reality you want, they also dramatically impact the resources, equipment and people that you'll need to make your dream come to life.

In short, your vision determines what financial targets and experiential outcomes you will have, which then determines what kind of resources you'll need to reach that target.

VISION ⟶ TARGET ⟶ HR/STAFF/ INFRASTRUCTURE NEEDS

Who Else Will Have Targets?

It's time to think like a CEO.

Even if you are a solo business owner working part time at home, you ARE running a business. The more you can think and act in the same way that the CEO of a Fortune 500 company would when planning their operations, the more success you will see.

One of the best ways to begin with this is to start thinking of your business as an entire organisation.

Start to create a visual picture of what 'departments' you have to manage and who else might be involved in each of these departments, bath now ad in the future.

ACTIVITY: Your Organisation

1. Using the example provided below, draw up your current organisation chart and add in names of people in each role - even if they are all you at present.
2. Draw up your ideal/goal organisation chart in 12 months time

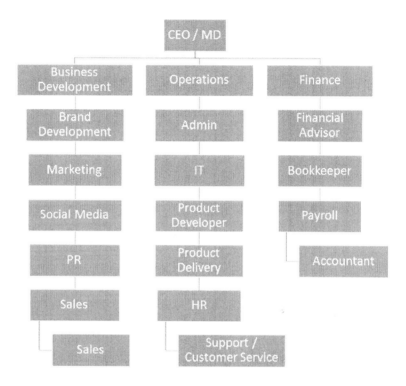

Define The Part They Play

If you were to hire a new employee, it would be impossible for them to do their life's best work, please you or meet their targets if they had absolutely no idea what they were expected to do.

People need clarity, parameters and direction – and so do you.

Humans get distressed and anxious when they cannot plan and prepare for their experiences. So if you do not know precisely where you are going or how you will get there, then you will experience a sense of unease, discomfort and dissatisfaction.

This stage is about writing up some clear job descriptions or duty statements for each of the roles that you have identified within your business – again, even if it is your name next to each role! Make sure that you know exactly what you should be doing when you are wearing that 'hat' and this will help you have clarity and focus when you are there – as well as give someone else a clear set of expectations when they take over from you.

If these roles are new to you and you are not sure what they are each supposed to do, then this is a much needed exercise for you! Start by first finding some 'generic' job descriptions online that you can use as a template.

Go to Google and type in the name of the role and 'job description template'. Open a handful of templates for each role, copy-paste a list of the duties and then contextualise them to suit your particular business.

You could even get a virtual assistant to do this initial template curating bit for you.

ACTIVITY: Define Your Roles

1. Create very detailed description of each of the positions shown in your 'organisation'
2. Write the top 5 'target's and outcomes of that job role in for the next 12 month period. What are the key results that they are going to bring to your business, or the success criteria that they are going to be assessed against in 12 months' time? This must be specific, such as an exact financial figure of income for example.
3. Now decide if you will be doing these roles yourself, if you will hire someone or outsource it.

If your business is going to work you are each of those employees until you replace yourself with somebody else!

As a word of warning, don't think that these roles are any less important or should be treated with any less formality just because you are doing them all yourself.

If you don't manage these roles when you are the identified personnel in the same way that you would manage them if an employee was doing them, your business will fail in just the same way it would if you employed somebody and expected them to perform without a job description, targets or management.

You wouldn't treat an employee with such disregard or wrist-flicking of unimportance, so don't allow neglect of the formality of your multiple roles to run your business either.

Setting Your Targets:

Your targets are vital.

Without a clear goal, you cannot possibly create a map to get there.

Earlier in this book I asked you to write down your financial goals for the coming 12 months.

Revisit that again now to make sure that it is still your target.

ACTIVITY: Target Planning

1. Write down the exact figure you want to make in the next 12 months in revenue
2. Divide that figure by 2080 (which is 40 x 52)
3. The result is what your time is worth per hour

You ideally shouldn't be working by the hour as discussed previously, but I want to bring your attention back to this as it places a benchmarking value on each of your business tasks which will help you decide which ones to eliminate, delegate or outsource in the upcoming stages of systemisation.

Next, estimate your figures VISION for the next 12 months:

4. What will be your revenue figure for each product or service in your business?
5. What will be your profit figures for each product or service in your business?
6. What will be your staff figures for each product or service in your business?

7. What will be your client figures for each product or service in your business?

Next, take these figures to create your sales TARGETS:

8. Sales figure by year:
9. Sales figure by quarter:
10. Sales figure by month:
11. Sales figure by week:
12. Sales figure by day:

Finally, now create 'KPI' statements for your business for the next 12 months

KPI means 'Key Performance Indicator' which are clearly defined, specific, measurable statements of exactly how much of something will be done or achieved in order to reach a certain objective.

Eg. If you want to make $1,000 per month and you sell $10 courses, then your KPI statement may be something like:

"I will sell 100 online courses at $10 per month so that I make an income of $1,000 per month"

Looking at your targets, how do you feel?

Hopefully you should be a little wowed, a little excited and also a little bit scared. If you are not scared by your targets, then they are not big enough.

I often take my targets and times them by 10.

Aside from being an ambitious person, I do this because our internal biology is there to 'protect' us; and so when it comes to goals, we will create ones that are 'safe' and 'predictable' – which usually means way within our comfort zones.

Don't be comfortable or you'll never grow.

Shoot for the stars and you might hit the moon, as they say.

Take your targets and times them by 10.

How Now?

Brilliant! We now have our goals and exact targets. The next destination point on the map has been marked and the compass has been set.

Now we need to work out how we are going to get there.

The 'how' is critical. Goals don't turn themselves into reality and no power of positive thinking will put your dreams on a plate.

Activity: How will you get there?

1. What methods will you use to achieve each goal?
2. What exact strategies will you use to get the outcomes you need?
3. What tasks must be completed in order to get the desired results?
4. Create an action plan of one-off, daily, weekly, monthly and quarterly tasks that you will conduct to reach the goals you have set for the next 12 months.

Conduct A Task Audit

Now you should have a pretty big action plan and to-do list.

The next thing you need to do is start to gather a big list of every other task within your business so that you have an overview of all of your business activity.

Open an excel sheet and list down every single task that:

1. You personally do
2. Your business does
3. Your staff or contractors do
4. Each product and service requires to be done
5. Each department needs to do

This list can seem pretty big and overwhelming at this stage, because yes, you guessed it, you are going to have to create a process and procedure for every single one!

But never fear, a lot will be removed before you do that.

Put this to one side as we are now going to build this out some more in the coming section.

Write Your Step By Step Instructions

Now that you have revisited your visions and set your targets, your next step is to put into place a clearly defined journey for the development and delivery of your product or service once it has been ordered or paid for.

Detail every single step that is taken by you, your staff and your customers.

What is the 'start trigger' of each process and what does the end to end journey look like in the delivery or production of this product or service?

You now need to write out the most detailed step by step instructions possible for everything that needs to be done in the purchasing, production and delivery process.

My rule is, that if a 10 year old child would struggle to follow your instructions, then they are not good enough.

Even if you never plan to take on staff, this process will give you a recipe for getting it right every time and enable you to see that actually, with a little time other people could actually do what you do too - instead of keeping yourself trapped in the futile mentality of *'only I can do this'.*

I call this stage 'The Franchise Model', whereby you create instructions and processes so robust, that you are able to duplicate the process over and over again. Multiplication enables you to scale into numerous geographical locations and employ any number of staff, and still get the same result for your customers.

No matter how 'bespoke' you think your services are, there are subtle processes and steps that you are going through every single time.

May be you start with a consult or strategy call.

What questions do you ask in those consults?

What information are you trying to obtain?

List out everything you would ask in every situation

Make one of those maps that has a series of questions with 'yes' and 'no' instruction flows that will formalise what feels like even the most complex of processes. There is a great tool call 'Lucid Chart' which I use for easily making visual processes that have lots of dependencies and layers.

Finally, add in training videos wherever possible. You can very cheaply and easily use screen capture software to record your computer screen to walk people through actual demonstrations and explanations as you go.

I personally use the Google platform (GSuite) to manage my entire business.

Here is an example of how I manage my company instructions:

How I Manage My Company Procedures

Task No#	Task Name	Notes/Comments	Who	Deadline
001				
002				
003				
004				

The 'hub' for my instructions and procedures is a Google Sheet (Google's version of an Excel sheet) and it also doubles up as my company 'To Do' list.

One of the things that I love most about the Google platform is that you can give different people different levels of permission to access, view and edit all documentation and multiple users can all access and edit the same document at the same time.

This sheet includes every single task that we have ever done, do all of the time and has all future tasks added to it too.

I give every single task a number, and the number hyperlinks to a Google Doc (Google's version of Word), where the detailed instructions are written out and demonstration videos have been embedded.

Instructions Template:

Keep a generic template for all of your internal procedures so that it's easy to follow.

My instructions include the following elements:

<Task Name> Procedure

Link to other documents you may need to reference here:
Document name: <link>

Video Instructions: <link>
Insert Video of the task being completed (training).
Keep videos under 5mins.
Simply upload your video to google drive, change share settings to 'whoever has the link can view' and insert the link here.

What
This is the process for: ....
(What is the result of this process)

When
This process is to commence when: ....
(What are the trigger points that will alert this person that the system needs to be followed)

Who

This procedure is to be completed by: ....
(What is the job title of the person performing this?)

How

- ☑ Checklist (a clear list of steps for implementation)
- ☑ List them in order
- ☑ Be explicitly clear
- ☑ Have them listed in check boxes like this, as it makes it clearer that they are steps to be followed in order.

Continue writing down what you do every day, creating a step by step instruction for that activity as if a child had to follow it and soon enough you'll have systems so robust that you'll be able to make yourself redundant!

Sarah's Hierarchy of Filtering Tasks

Now that you have your tasks lists, let's see what we can take off of our burden, lighten the load and have you only focusing on the high value tasks.

Time to audit everything, measure it next to our 'hourly rate' to see if each task is worth our personal time doing, or if it is in fact more profitable to hire someone else to do it.

For instance, if you have decided that you want your annual turnover to be $500,000 a year, then you need to be earning $240 an hour.

So why would you spend 8 hours mucking around with trying to make some posters for your event (wasting $1,920 of your time), that would have cost you only $20 for a freelancer to do for you?

This next stage is about getting realistic with what you are putting your time into and how you are managing your tasks.

For every single task in your list, you are now going to ask yourself the following questions in this order:

1. Can you **ELIMINATE** it? If yes, then delete it. If not, move to the next stage.
2. Can you **AUTOMATE** it? If yes, set up the automation. If not, move to the next stage.
3. Can you **OUTSOURCE** it? If yes, find your contractors. If not, then move to the next stage.
4. Can you **DELEGATE** it? If yes, delegate it. If not, then move to the next stage.
5. Are you *SURE* that you are the ONLY person that can do this? Are you absolutely POSITIVE that there is no other way of doing this? If yes, then add it to your personal list. If there is another way of doing it, do it the other way!

I will further extrapolate on each of these hierarchical stages now:

Eliminate

The next stage of systemising your business model is to then look at everything you do to sell, produce and deliver your product or service and then decide what can be eliminated. Sometimes we have steps we do not need, or options we give our customers that just cause confusion, or resources that are not required - even tasks we do ourselves that are not really required.

Delete everything and anything that is not absolutely critical to the process.

Just get rid of it.

Automate

Automation has been huge in my ability to take on more customers, create more consistent customer experiences and ultimately scale my business.

By using automation tools such as online order forms, online quote request forms, online payment forms, a customer record management system, automated email sequences and a combination of online apps, I have been able to replace people - including myself - in many parts of my business in a way that has significantly improved my customer experience.

By using technology instead of people, you can remove inconsistent operations, ensure that business is being taken care of 24/7, never have to worry about holidays, weekends, sick days, bad moods, pay rises or international time zones and also massively reduce your overheads.

Outsource

You may have identified parts of your business that require human input, skill and talent.

But before defaulting to *'if I want it done properly, then I should do it myself'*; or *'Oh no, now I have to train people in something I'm not amazing at myself'*, first consider outsourcing.

There are freelancers, contractors, small businesses and companies who specialise in every type of skill you could imagine.

People who have dedicated their entire lives, education, professions and business resources to that thing you need done and if you look around hard enough you will find people willing to work on an 'as needs basis', meaning that you get professional work done without the stress or the overheads.

Outsourcing means sending it to somebody else to do.

There are lots of ways to outsource.

The cheapest ways are to find freelancers on sites such as Upwork.com, where people from every industry you could imagine, with every skill you could wish for, are there to offer you their services as required.

You post your 'job' with a full description and a budget, and freelancers will bid against one another to get your post.

You can also outsource to other businesses who may specialise their entire suite of services around that one thing that you need.

Outsourcing can be hard to find the right people and takes a little getting used to. Like any form of 'employment', outsourcing requires you to know precisely what you want first, and then to implement a process of selection, onboarding and off boarding.

Start Small and Slow

Get freelancers to first do a trial job for you and get more than one to do the trial – pay them for the trial. Base their skills on what they show you that they can do, not on what they say that they can do.

Secondly, when it comes to finding 'experts', make sure you check out a few things before you get fooled by any false claims.

- Experts have at least 5 years demonstrable experience in their area of expertise and can back that up with historical evidence, customer testimonials, a portfolio of work, published work.
- They have recognised qualifications and formal training in their area of expertise.

- These days it's also worth looking for a website and social media presence – if they can't afford it or can't be bothered with it, it tells me a lot about how seriously they take their business – and their customers business.

What Not To Outsource

Outsourcing has certainly changed my business, but make sure you do it in the right places with the right people.

Things I do NOT outsource are my social media (excluding advertising), or content creating such as blogs, books and courses – courses because that is my own area of expertise, but the others because these are your 'voice'.

The way you speak, write and communicate say everything about who you are and can only be uniquely you.

Nobody else can capture your essence other than you.

So my personal advice is that if you don't like writing, don't outsource it, instead learn how to get comfortable on camera and do videos that you can later get transcribed and edited by an outsourcer; or do audio recordings or use the Google Voice Recording tool to dictate out your written content through speech.

But don't ever give someone else the power to take your voice and your most powerful relationship building tool from you.

It is your voice that will attract those most like you, and therefore the 'perfect match' customers for your personality and style.

Get someone else to 'speak' for you, and you'll be attracting people that connect with 'their' voice, not yours – and that is not a good thing.

Believe in yourself, you are capable of learning every skill in the world.

However, for everything else – find a good collection of people who can do it for you.

Your life will never be the same when you master outsourcing, but ease into it with the same level of caution that you'd apply to employing a full time legal employee so that you don't make any rash decisions on the wrong partners.

Delegate

Sometimes outsourcing is not an option.

There could be an onsite requirement, a multidisciplinary team that need to be together or privacy and security issues that require an on-location, employee based delivery.

In which case, before taking on any tasks yourself, first see if you can delegate it to someone else.

If it is something that will need to be done more than once ever again in the foreseeable existence of your life, then take the time to write up some epic instructions for the task or role, and then take someone on and give them the opportunity to do their life's best work through some good training.

ACTIVITY: Finalising Your Systems

Now that you understand each of the actions that you can apply to deal with each task, go back to your list of tasks and finish your 'Task Audit' that you started earlier in this section.

Make another column in your tasks list (processes and procedures list) against every item on your list and write one of the following letters based on what you can do with that task:

E: Eliminate

A: Automate

O: Outsource

D: Delegate

K: Keep Doing

Keep Doing

The final stage of the task filtering hierarchy, is the 'keep doing' stage.

This method may only be used if there is absolutely no way whatsoever that it can be done in any other of the ways listed in the previous stages.

This is stuff that only you can do, such as high level strategic planning, the 'you' specific client consults or flagship IP courses, workshops and public speaking. It could be writing your blog posts, writing books, filming your educational videos and sales videos as the 'face' of your business.

Of course these are not the only things that could fall under you, but make sure that there really is no way that this could not be replicated. Even sales calls can be outsourced.

When items fall into this stage of 'you need to do it yourself', then make sure that you are charging for it accordingly.

This is the highest end of the spectrum in my pricing model (which I describe in a later section) as you are exchanging your personal time as 'done *with* you' or 'done *for* you' and thus are top of the price range.

Remember your hourly rate? This better be that multiplied by a lot, because this is where the activity you are applying yourself to gets the absolute best of you and your brilliant mind.

And that brings us to the end of this chapter on systemising.

Use your online courses and other educational products and services to lead your customers into all of the other ways that you can continue to serve them; then create solid systems that form a predictable production line, profit margin, customer experience and enable you to scale.

Final Chapter Checklist:

- Write up your vision, mission and goals
- Write up your business sales and income targets
- Write up your KPI's & core outputs for the next 12 months
- Write up your list of income generating products & services
- Conduct a task assessment
- Draw your organisational chart

- Write up your detailed job descriptions
- Conduct your task automation & outsourcing allocation
- Write up your detailed task systems, processes & procedures for every task
- Formalise your review, analysis and continuous improvement plan

STAGE 10: SCALE

The ultimate stage of a well designed business, and one that will attract a much higher value for sale, is one that has the ability to scale.

However, it's not everybody's dream to create a large company; so why do it?

Some people started a small business because of the fact that it enables them to just be on their own and do their own thing the way they want to do it.

Therefore, when I say "scalability", I don't necessarily mean growing it into a conglomerate or taking on a team the size of a village and becoming an IPO.

When I say "scalability", what I mean is your ability to take on more customers without necessarily doing more work.

Wouldn't you like to design a business that has the capacity to grow in turn-over, profit and number of people you have provided a positive experience to, without you necessarily working any harder than you are now?

More money for less work? Of course you're interested! This is what scaling (especially when married with automation) is about.

Regardless of whether you are a solo business owner, or have a huge team, when the amount of your output is directly proportionate to your number of hours in a day, or number of human heads at a desk, then your scalability is limited significantly.

Let's look at an example just to make this clear. I own a training organisation, and when it was purely traditional face-to-face training and nothing else, the amount of income I made was largely dependent on the number of hours in a day, the size of the training rooms available and the number of training staff that I had on my books. If I wanted to make more money, I had to hire more staff.

This is scalable only to the number of suitable Trainers that I can find in my topic in my area, that are free on the days I needed them for the budget that I had…. which is NOT very scalable.

The bigger the client list, the bigger the resources I needed, which is NOT what scaling properly is.

Here's a more scalable example.

Later, I put all of our professional development filming online. I was able to take my fulltime employees from 23 down to 1. My client capacity went from 15-20 students in a room, to a limitless number.

This meant that my income went from a limited amount, to an unlimited amount – whilst simultaneously removing hundreds of thousands of dollars in overheads, and completely getting rid of the problems and responsibilities that comes with a physically large business.

I could keep on adding courses (products), keep on increasing my client base (self-enrolled, self-study students), increasing my income (especially since many were signing up for the subscription offering) – all whilst DECREASING my workload.

That, is what you call scaling.

What could you do to start scaling your business?

CHAPTER 5

HOW TO PRICE YOUR COURSES, PRODUCTS & SERVICES

How much should you be charging for your educational products and programs?

Wouldn't it be nice if there was a simple answer for that? But you have probably learned by now that being an edupreneur isn't always easy, and learning how to price your wares is one of those challenges.

There are an enormous amount of dependable 'what-if's' and variables that come into the pricing of your courses, products and services, which makes this impossible to give a one-liner answer to.

Similarly, no single answer would ever be able to apply to every reader of this book.

So instead of giving you answers, I am going to ask you some questions to begin with.

ACTIVITY: How Much Are You Worth?

1. How much are you worth?

   As in, how much would you have paid someone to have all of the answers and strategies that you have, back when you needed them most?

Imagine if the 'present day' version of yourself went back in time to give the 'inexperienced' version of you a complete brain download and hard drive of everything you needed to skip all of the long winded learning curve and skip straight to the 'present day' version of yourself. What would the 'inexperienced' you be willing to pay the 'experienced expert' version of you for this help and guidance?

Write down an actual figure.

2. If you are doubting whether you have value to give, go back and remind yourself where you once were and what you would give to have skipped past all of the hard, long winded lessons that you went through to get where you are now.

    What would that be worth?

3. Check the outcomes your courses, products and services are going to provide.

    Can you calculate what savings your learners will be making by taking the short cuts that you offer? This could include saving making costly mistakes, saving in time costs, saving in expensive programs etc.

    That is another figure to work with.

4. Can you calculate the value or income that your teachings, products and services could give to your customers as a result of investing in them? If so, what is that figure?

There is still a lot more to explore in terms of pricing, but hopefully this exercise helps you see that what you have to offer is both extremely valuable and in many ways priceless.

Never undersell yourself.

Keep these higher figures in mind as we now go through the rest of this chapter.

"What you have to offer is both extremely valuable and in many ways priceless.

Never undersell yourself"

Cost Analysis

The first place to begin when it comes to determining your pricing, is to start with knowing what your overheads are.

If you sell a product or service for less than it costs you to produce and deliver it, then you'll be making a loss and will go broke very quickly.

You need to make profit in order to be able to run a business; and the bigger that profit the better.

ACTIVTIY: Your Break-Even Point

So first, create a cost outline sheet which breaks down every single expense you have in building, selling and hosting your online courses, products and services.

Don't forget to include expenses such as:

- software
- storage
- contractors
- employees (including their taxes, super and insurances)
- time taken to train staff and contractors
- taxes
- apps
- insurances
- physical goods
- your own time (development, production and maintenance)
- equipment
- resources
- rent
- even costs of utilities such as the electric that kept your laptop running, and;
- the price of the coffee that fueled you through the production process.

Now calculate all of these expenses for your estimated production and delivery process (an estimation is better than nothing – and *always overestimate by at least 10%* so that you have some buffer room.

Overestimating will win you profit.

Underestimating will result in a loss.

This calculation will give you your 'cost' figure.

When you have the 'cost' figure, now you have the price that your product or service cannot be less than – or your 'break even' mark.

Calculate your 'break even' mark for every product and service that you offer (or plan to).

Don't forget that the final price of your product or service is going to need to be higher than your cost price, or you won't ever be making a profit and will spend your life working for free!

OR – for passively sold products, make sure that you have a short term and small volume of sales that will cover your initial expenses quickly and return your investment quickly.

Eg, let's pretend it costs me $500 to produce and publish an online course, and I sell that online course for $147. I know that I have to sell at least 4 courses before I have re-acquired my costs and start making a profit. I also know that every single sale after the 4th one will be 100% profit.

Benchmark the Market

Once you have answered the initial questions and got your 'break even' figure, the next most logical step to ascertaining your pricing is to check out the competition.

As part of the research phase you should have gathered data on what competing courses, products and services look like and sell for in your industry.

The trick here is not to copy others prices and products – as not only is this grossly unethical, but worse, you would be simply building yourself a battle field of competing products.

Instead, notice the trends and determine where your unique place is in your market using those top and bottom price points as an indicator of what your market are willing to pay. Never assume however that you need to 'fit inside' these figures. These are only showing you what other people are charging for their courses and content, not what people would be willing to pay for yours. So make sure you stay focused on the outcomes that your course provides, not 'what everyone else is doing'.

As you are checking out the competition also consider your breakeven price point based on your expenses.

If the average competing product or service on the market is priced considerably lower than your break-even mark, you may have to go back to the drawing board on your production process or even your entire offering idea, as this simple information shows that you may price yourself out of the market before you've even made a profit.

The prices you see in the market shouldn't keep you restricted within those variances however. As much as they are a guide as to what people expect to pay for product and services like yours, remember that yours is *different*, that you are different and the *results* your customers will get from your offerings will be different to what they'd get from the others is different too.

My advice is to always find ways of creating something *better* than what is currently on the market so that you can price HIGHER than the competition, never lower.

Know Your Revenue To Unit Breakdown

Earlier on in this book, I asked you to define what your goal revenue is for the next 12 months. If you now know what you want to earn, the next step for commercialising and creating a profitable business model is to then decide how you will attain that revenue to the detail of each sold unit of stock, product or service.

Are you going to price your offerings low and go for large volumes of sales?

The $1 razor club chose this model, selling razors for just $1. Yet in 2016, sold for $1 BILLION!! Low priced products does not necessarily mean low revenue – so long as profit and volume exceed costs.

You could also choose to sell much higher priced offerings so that you have less customers but a high revenue.

Of course there is absolutely no right or wrong to this at all. It all comes down to the type of life, business, customers and income you want to have.

Planning what your price point vs effort will be will dramatically influence the way your entire business operates.

11 Ways to make $1 Million

Let's pretend that your revenue goal is to make $1 million in the next 12 months.

Which way of earning $1million most tantalises your taste buds the most?

1. 1 x client @ $1,000,000
2. 2 x clients @ $500,000 each
3. 5 x clients @ $200,000 each
4. 10 x clients @ $100,000 each
5. 50 x clients @ $20,000 each
6. 100 x clients @ $10,000 each
7. 500 x clients @ $2,000 each
8. 1,000 x clients @ $1,000 each
9. 5,000 x clients @ $200 each
10. 10,000 clients @ $100 each
11. 1,000,000 clients x $1 each

Each of these would require a focus on very different markets, approaches to market, the types of products and services on offer and how they would be delivered.

However, the purpose here is to figure out if you are going to go for low value offerings to a mass market, or high value offerings to a niche market?

Sarah's Value Pricing Model

You should now be starting to build an informed picture about what price you need to be selling at to meet your overheads, to make a profit, to meet the industry expectations and to also meet your own revenue vs effort objectives.

Now it's time to also take a look at the type of content, product or service you are offering to further assess it's value and subsequent price point.

This model is not only important for your pricing, but forms the structure of any good edupreneurial business model.

Great businesses understand that all of their consumers are different and want to consume your information in different ways.

Just as some love to hear your educational content in audio format such as Podcasts and MP3s, some like to watch the same content as videos, others prefer to read, some like to be face to face in a room with you, others just like it done for them and others like to have their hand held personally by you and learn how it's done one on one. As they select each of these different types of content, they move through an increasing price bracket.

I will not give actual figures for each of these stages because there is no 'right' answer and there are too many variables per industry and offering.

However, here is an overview of how the price of your courses, products and services could be affected based on where in my *Value Pricing Model* that they fit.

Here is my 'Value Pricing Model':

Information: $-$$
Implementation: $$-$$$
Transformation: $$$-$,$$$
Do It For You: $,$$$-$$,$$$
Do It With You: $$,$$$-$$$,$$$

Do not be 'literal' with the number of dollar signs I have used next to each one. This is illustrative of 'lowest price' to 'highest price', not necessarily actual dollar digits to charge at each stage.

Let's now explore each of these stages in a little more detail so that you can start to apply my model to your own business.

Breakdown of The Value Stages

Information: $-$$

The 'information' stage is the lowest price point, where your offering is most likely to be free, or the smallest entry point for pricing – such as the $1 - $50 mark.

This is the lowest priced because 'information' is often freely available anywhere. It's what any good edupreneur is sharing freely daily in many different formats to ensure that they are demonstrating their expertise and building a relationship with their audience.

In my business model, this stage includes my podcasts (my own and guest speaking on other people's), blogs, eBooks, YouTube videos, many free and $10 online courses, free in-person talks that I give at events and workshops organised by other people, downloads, cheat sheets, livestreams and social media posts.

ACTIVITY: List 10 things that you could do or give for free (or very low priced) to demonstrate your expertise and attract the perfect audience.

Implementation: $$-$$$

Implementation takes us to a higher price point in our course pricing model. This is because this is the stage where we go beyond simple information and provide people with strategies, recipes and step by step processes; essentially the 'how' and 'what to do' to get the result that they are after.

In my experience the average online course will fit into this category.

ACTIVITY: List 10 things that you could create, offer or publish that would fit into the implementation content level, and what you would charge for them.

Transformation: $$$-$,$$$

This is the stage where your product or service does more than just provide people with skills, tools, knowledge and recipes. This is the stage where they themselves, or the life they experience measurably changes as a result.

Perhaps they got healthier, happier, richer, freer, more confident – the list could go on forever! But the point is that the transformation stage is a product or service that undeniably moves somebody from point 'A' to point 'B' after it has been delivered, and as such their life is transformed in some way.

ACTIVITY: List 10 ways that you transform people's lives, bodies, businesses (anything!). How do you make people and the lives they live *different* after they have worked with you?

Do It For You: $,$$$-$$,$$$

No matter how amazing your online courses, books, podcasts, keynote presentations or face to face workshops are, there are people out there who simply just want it done for them.

They want to ease and simplicity of handing it all over to an expert, avoiding the learning curve and just getting the job done. They understand that this 'hands off' approach for them means paying a higher fee, but would rather that than do it themselves.

What do you teach? How can you turn that into a 'done for you' service?

ACTIVITY: List 10 things that you do every day for yourself, or teach regularly that you could consider turning into a 'done for you' service – and even hiring a team to do under you.

Do It With You: $$,$$$-$$$,$$$

This is your ultimate, premium offering as you, the expert, are going to completely give yourself in person to your client. You will treat them like a VIP and hold absolutely nothing back in sharing your expertise and knowledge with them in person.

You will provide everything above, including information, implementation and total transformation and do it all under the most personal of experiences.

My versions of this are my 'Course Creation Bootcamps' and my 'One Day Set Up Service' (if you want to have a look at what I include in these services as an example, you can get all of the info here: www.sarahcordiner.com/services).

In my Course Creation Bootcamps I include luxury accommodation in a private villa and limit the number of attendees to 10. This means that we all live together under one roof (jokingly referred to as 'The Big Brother House'!) for the ultimate immersion course creation experience. There is always a swimming pool, sometimes spa's, we've even hired full time maids and private chefs on some of our Bootcamps!

There are no topics off limits, no 'finish times' to my 'top end' service. It's 24 hour access to me personally as a friend, a housemate and a teacher; to my team and my film crew.

My 'One Day Set Up Service' goes one step further than that.

I invite my client to stay at my own personal home with me for the night and spend the next day planning and filming their online course. I take them out for a luxurious dinner the night before, we sit in my garden and chat about their business into the night and then we film and course create like crazy together one on one the next day. I personally collect them and drop them off at the airport and make them breakfast and lunch in my own kitchen. ... and the list goes on.

This is simply an example of how I personally have taken one area of expertise (course creation), and turned it into multiple income streams, from $5 self-study online courses, right the way through to high-end, luxury experiences.

This top level of your offerings is the ultimate personal experience and where the utmost amount of value can be given to your client. It's more than a service or a course, it's an unforgettable and life-changing experience.

ACTIVITY: What kind of 'done with you' experiences could you offer? Brainstorm 3 ways that you could create a high value 'with you' experience.

Based on the level of transformation, tools and experience you plan to provide, what price points do you anticipate to charge for your higher end 'done with you' services?

"*Your highest value offerings need to be more than just 'services' or 'training'.*

They need to be unforgettable, life-changing experiences."

Picking The Perfect Payment Options

There are a number of different ways that you can charge for your online courses, products and services today, and they are made super simple by online learning platforms, which I will go into in the coming chapters.

These include:

- Fixed one off payments
- Payment plans
- Subscriptions
- Multi-product pricing
- Bulk purchase pricing

Fixed One-Off Payments

This is simply setting a fixed price for your course, charging said amount and allowing your user to have access to that training for the time period that you specified in your sales description or terms and conditions.

Payment Plans

This method works well for your higher priced courses, where the price might be a barrier to some due to not having that amount available as a disposable amount in one go.

The payment plan option works by you setting the price for your online course, and then deducting a set amount from the customers' credit card, at a set frequency, for a set period of time until the full amount is paid off.

You can even 'drip release' your online course content so that the user only gets access to the portions that they have paid for to date so that you can protect your income and assets.

Subscriptions

A subscription is when you charge a recurring price for your learners to access your course(s).

This could be simply charging $10 a month for one single online course, a little more for a small handful of courses, or hundreds per month for access to an entire suite of courses.

From a purely commercial point of view, the subscription payment method is my favourite, as subscriptions mean consistent cash flow.

When I was only selling my online courses for 'one off' prices, my income fluctuated quite a lot from month to month depending on what marketing, promotions or exposure I'd worked on that month.

However, when I added a subscription option to my courses, slowly my monthly income has started to not only increase, but become more predictable each time. A predictable cash flow means a healthy business and so I personally encourage all course creators to include (or plan on including) a subscription offering for their online courses.

A subscription is very easy to set up in your learning management system, the learner agrees to the automatic deductions from their account when they sign up and can cancel their membership at any time themselves; reducing your administration.

Because subscriptions are so favourable to your bottom line, my advice is to make your subscription offering a total no-brainer, so that your customers choose that option over any other.

As a REAL example, at the time of writing this page, I had over 40 (publicly accessible) online courses in my online academy. The individual one-off prices for each of those courses range from $25 to over $1,000 each and collectively are worth thousands.

However, what I did to attract people to entering into a subscription to my school instead of making unpredictable one off payments, was to make an offer that was absolutely crazy for them not to take.

As well as having the one off pricing available, in addition, I created a 'bundle' of over 40 of my online courses, and I set it to just $47 a month – cancel anytime – subscription.

I made it very clear that they would get immediate, full access to all of the 40+ courses from the instant that they paid the first $47.

I even told them in the sales description that they can 'binge watch all of the courses and then cancel the subscription and thus get thousands of dollars worth of training for just $47'.

I then strategically placed the '$47 Get Everything' bundle as the very first product in my online academy; so that everything that the learners look at after that will be compared to '40 courses for just $47'.

Why would they pay $297 for a course, when it's included in the $47 deal? So of course, they begin signing up for the $47 deal in droves.

Later I will add more courses to this bundle and increase the monthly subscription price for new users and offer the existing member an upgrade option to get access to the new courses, or just keep their 'old' library for the same amount. Due to the psychological effects of 'FOMO' (fear of missing out), I'm pretty confident that the majority of subscribers will upgrade.

It might seem strange to make such an insane offer – especially when I've just spent so much effort telling you to price high and not devalue your content!

However, when you are shifting models, you not only have a market's mindset to transition, you also have a volume-based mindset to shift too.

Because of the fact that I have high-end services, I personally use my online courses as my 'bottom of funnel' low priced offerings. (This won't be the case for everyone's business model, but for me it works).

This means, that it is 'safe' for me to keep my course prices lower and to go for the 'mass market' approach rather than the 'niche market' approach – which is reserved for my high end services.

Sensational Subscriptions

"But I don't want to sell all of my courses for just $47 Sarah!" I hear you scream. So don't. I'm not telling anyone that you should do this, or for this amount, I'm simply sharing one of my models to inspire you and open up your mind to ideas of other ways that you could be increasing your income with your edu-products; because increasing your income they do!

Just as an example, here is a little Math on the passive recurring income potential on a simple $47 a month subscription model:

10 students = $470 per month

50 students = $2,350 per month

100 students = $4,700 per month

150 students = $7,050 per month

250 students = $11,750 per month

750 students = $35,250 per month

1,000 students = $47,000 per month

1,500 students = $70,500 per month

2,500 students = $117,500 per month

5,000 students = $235,000 per month

10,000 students = $470,000 per month

Not so bad now, eh?

To add another layer to the subscription model, when applied to corporate learning, this can become exceptionally profitable to you – whilst providing HUGE savings to and flexible learning options to your clients' company.

Work out how many people they need to immediately train for one course, and instead of charging them a fixed rate per head for that one course, offer them a monthly subscription for unlimited staff to access all of your online courses for a fixed period.

They will be saving thousands over paying per course per head, and you will be making thousands for proving the solution.

Everyone's a winner!

Multi-Product Pricing

Multi-product pricing is another great way to increase the value that you are providing to your customers, as well as the price you can charge, by combining a number of your products and services into one single offer – right from within your online school!

As an example, instead of just having the online course for a set price, you could include an eBook (as a download or PDF lecture), you could add a live skype consult with you and a checklist. This will increase your price per head sale – and could of course take payment for this one off, as a payment plan or even as a subscription!

Not only is your online school a great place to host and deliver these items, it also takes care of the payment processing for you too.

Bulk Purchase Pricing

Bulk pricing works best for organisations and groups of buyers.

For example, you may have an online course topic that would be attractive to corporates, larger businesses with staff, Government and agencies.

You could offer a price per head, or offer multiple pricing options based on the number of places they purchase on your online course. I slightly decrease the price per head as the volume of places increases so that it incentivises these clients to buy the larger pack of user access to my courses.

If you go to my online academy you will be able to see how I have set this up if you select on the 'Employability' courses category.

Test The Market But Remember That You Are In Charge

Now that you have based your starting point on some solid foundations of cost covering and the level of value that you are delivering, the next check in is going to be with the market themselves.

Don't wait until you have a perfectly produced and completed product before you go out to the market to check what they might pay for your program. You can approach your market and share your planned course, product or service offering with them and ask them what they would pay if they were looking for a service like that. You could even have some fun and make it a 'guess the price' competition. See what people pick as the 'expected' price and then make sure you reward everyone who entered with a thank you gift for helping you – such as a discounted access to the course when it's ready or another product that you can share freely.

If you are going to offer discounts and coupons for your courses, always make sure you start at the lowest sale price (maximum discount) and slowly increase the minimum price (reducing the discount amount). You want to reward early purchasers and pre-buyers with big discounts.

Never launch at a high price and then later down the line offer big discounts – this will really upset people who have paid full price in the past, as well as suggest that you have 'unwanted stock'. A bit like the end of season sales in shopping malls, or the 'bargain bucket' outside of supermarkets – you know it's all the junk that they couldn't sell or is about to expire. Constant discounting can do this to your courses and people will hold off on purchasing your new programs in case you discount it later if they see that you are someone who decreases your pricing over time.

Keep adding content to your courses so that you can justify a continued increase in price. This is actually easier than it sounds as you will find that once you have a handful of students in your course, that they will start asking lots of different questions. These questions simply become the source for more course content. As soon as you've filmed the answer as an instructional video and uploaded it, increase the course price accordingly.

This way you will find that your course (and other edu-products and services) can go up higher and higher over time to reflect the increasing value. Only when you reach a point at which the sales begin to reduce, should you stop increasing the price. The market will tell you when too much is too much.

Don't ever be tempted to 'do what everyone else is doing'. Your courses, your services, your business, the outcomes that your students get – are all very different to that which your competitors have (or at least should be so that you have a point of difference and are not competing directly with them.

Despite all of this information, ultimately as a business owner and product producer, you always get the final choice over what you sell your wares and services for.

Value yourself, value your experience, give value and charge what you believe is an honest and fair exchange for the content, product or service that you have created.

No matter what any marketer, business guru or course creation chick like me tells you, remember that YOU always, always get the final say.

CHAPTER 6

WHERE & HOW TO SELL YOUR ONLINE COURSES FOR MAXIMUM SALES AND EXPOSURE

There are a number of different ways that you can sell online courses and there are quite literally thousands of platforms out there that you can use to sell your online course from.

However, all of these thousands of platforms generally fit into one of 3 main categories which I will explain in this section.

Just like anything, they all have their unique benefits and limitations.

Once you understand the differences, pros and cons of each one, you'll be well on your way to milking all of the benefits and maximising your sales and exposure.

The Three Main Ways To Host And Sell Your Online Courses

1. Online course marketplaces
2. Learning Management System (LMS)
3. Website plugins / software

Which one should you be using and what do they mean? Read on...

Platform 1: Online Course Marketplaces

Online course marketplaces are the 'supermarkets' of the online course world.

These platforms are privately owned, but open to the world. They welcome selling products from others and will provide the shoppers for you to some degree. They price their products low, but the volume opportunity is high.

Let's keep using this supermarket analogy to help you understand the real value (and warnings) of the online course marketplace platform.

A traditional supermarket that sells your groceries is often very well known, has strong marketing, is visited regularly by it's customers and has a high volume of customers.

A supermarket sells multiple products by multiple different brands and businesses, even if there are lots of the 'same' types of products on one shelf. Because of the fact that so many shoppers are coming through the door, each with their different needs, tastes and preferences, it doesn't matter too much that there might be 10 different brands of bread, or 6 different brands of tuna. Everyone makes a sale.

If you were selling groceries in that supermarket, people might buy your product even if they didn't intend to when they walked in.

There's a lot of spontaneous buying that happens in supermarkets. How many times have you thrown something in your trolley that you had no previous intention of buying before you went into the supermarket?

The same principles apply to the online course marketplaces.

You get to put your online course on a 'supermarket shelf' – a supermarket that specialises in selling online courses, and already has MILLIONS of online course shoppers strolling up and down the aisles actively browsing for the next course to catch their eye.

They might have been looking for a course on Microsoft Excel, but end up buying your course on parenting, just because they saw it there.

One of the biggest online course marketplaces out there right now is Udemy.com who currently have over 17 MILLION students registered on their platform who are all looking for, buying and enrolling in online courses. That's 17 million potential customers that you are missing out on if you do not have your online courses on there.

17 million potential customers that somebody else has done all of the work to bring through the doors for you.

In short, this is the biggest benefit to marketplaces. If you are not on the shelf, you are missing out on shoppers, it's as simple as that.

However, all that shines is not made of gold – so of course there is a 'but'.

When it comes to supermarkets who do you think has control over the price of the product on that supermarket shelf? It's going to be the supermarket.

If the supermarket decides to do a big discount sale, who do you think decides what price your product gets sold for? The supermarket.

If the supermarket decides to change the branding or move the shelves around, they can decide that – AND they take a very big percentage of every course sale you make. After all, they are giving you a fully functioning and maintained platform for free and provided 17 million+ students for you – it's kind of fair that they get a return for that! This is their business – would you work for free?

The effort they put into providing the platform is huge. In July 2017 I was the Media Correspondent for 'Udemy Live', Udemy's annual instructor conference in San Francisco.

As part of my role I was granted all-access free reign to the Udemy Head Quarters in San Francisco and aside from being blown away by what wonderful people work at Udemy; I was utterly stunned by the size of the operations there. It took me an entire day to get round each department and interview some of the Heads. I could have got lost in there for weeks! When you realise how much expense and expertise goes into providing a platform like this, you become extremely grateful for it and happily exchange some commission to have it – after all, you wouldn't be earning anything at all from Udemy if Udemy didn't exist!

Anyway, going back to some of the considerations you need to be aware of, Udemy naturally have rules that must be followed to ensure that their brand is protected in the process of giving you a leg up to share your content with the world under their name.

Your online course must meet certain criteria in terms of length, content type, audio quality and visual quality among some other branding requirements. Your sales pages need to be written a certain way and you have no control over refund requests.

So, when it comes to online course marketplaces I want you to have this 'supermarket' analogy in mind.

You do not get control over the pricing of your course, you don't necessarily get control over the discounting that happens to the price of your course.

You also don't own the students that are taking your course, because the online course marketplace owns the customers – not you.

If you don't own the customers, and your courses get discounted heavily and there are so many rules to follow in an online course marketplace, then would you use them?

Remember the 17 million students?

Why wouldn't you want to put your amazing product in front of these people that otherwise wouldn't even know that you exist?

And importantly, why wouldn't you do this when you actually get *paid* for that exposure?

The way I like to see online course marketplaces is as a way to give to the world, to share my message with the world, to promote and market myself, to get exposure to people I wouldn't have, whilst getting paid for it.

In my opinion, anyone not strategically using online course marketplaces is completely bonkers and seriously missing out!

A lot of people will happily *spend* money on Facebook ads with full knowledge that they may not get any return at all for their ad spend.

Marketplaces might sell my courses for a low price, but I'm still getting paid for it. I'm still get paid to get exposure to a brand new market that someone else is doing the work for.

Unlike the person pouring buckets of money into Facebook ads who is betting their money on what is essentially a high risk gamble; the course creators who are using online course marketplaces as a paid form of marketing are getting 100% profits from their 'marketing' activity.

I encourage people to think of the online course marketplace almost as the bottom of their funnel.

Take a sample of your 'Big Mumma' online course – such as a smaller, condensed version, or a taster of your full online course, and put that on these open marketplaces. That way, it won't impact the value of your course if it is sold at a high discount as it is only a portion of the full course.

Of course, make sure it's a good mini course that will give your learners a tangible outcome. If they didn't enjoy your mini course, they certainly won't want to take your 'advanced' version.

The advanced version by the way, will NOT be hosted on the marketplace – this is where another platform comes in, such as the LMS or the plugin – discussed next.

For it's when people from the marketplaces are so wowed by you and your content that they want more from you and will willingly search for you or purchase anything else that you offer them that this models starts to bring in the magic.

If you are a smart course creator, the next thing you offer the marketplace students will be something that is hosted in your own 'boutique' store. On land that you own, can control and where the customer and their data also becomes yours too.

Use marketplaces because:

Millions of students ready and waiting to buy online courses like yours, so you get mass exposure – fast. The potential to get very large student numbers here is extremely high too.

All of the technology, maintenance and admin is handled by the marketplace – all you have to do is upload

Quick and easy set up with big support groups and lots of free training

There are hundreds, even thousands of online promotion websites and social media groups that are dedicated to promoting online courses hosted on marketplaces; so even if you do plan to do marketing yourself it is very easy when you are hosted on a marketplace

You can place your smaller online courses on the marketplaces and direct your marketplace learners to your 'advanced course versions' that are hosted on your own private platforms *(**always check the marketplace self-promotion rules before you do this)*

Platform 2: Learning Management Systems

The 'Learning Management System' is known in the industry as the 'LMS'.

This is the equivalent of your own 'boutique store', in comparison to the supermarket. I call mine my 'online school' or 'online academy'.

A LMS is different from a marketplace because you've bought or rented the land yourself – you are the landlord, you've built your own little boutique shop, and it's all yours.

Therefore, when people walk into your shop you may communicate with them and build a relationship with them however you wish. You may offer them whatever you wish and present them with whatever products and services you wish in any way you wish, for whatever exchange you wish.

If they choose to give you their personal details, then you get to keep those details yourself. That customer belongs to you. You get their email address, you get to deliver that product to them however you want, you get to choose the pricing of your products, you get to choose your discounting, your special offers, your big fat promotion days and all of the branding.

YOU are in complete control of your own LMS, no one else can dictate or control what you do in there.

The downside (for some) is that you have to do your own marketing when you have your own LMS.

It's like having your own WordPress website. You bought the software and you own it in every way; and because it is your business, nobody is going to grow your business for you.

Because you own this space, this is where you're going to put your full courses, your higher end courses, your more expensive programs. Your LMS is the heart of your education-based business. You can even sell your eBooks, coaching and more from your LMS, as like a website, you have a lot of freedom over how you 'design' it and what you put on it.

Similarly to marketplaces, LMSs have been designed to be 'click and go'. They have become so simple to use that even the most tech-fearing newbie can quickly and easily build and sell a course by following the logical step by step, build as you go user interfaces.

Your PayPal and Stripe (free payment tools) are integrated with your LMS at the click of a button as they are already built with these features embedded.

The 'pretty landing pages' are all pre-designed for you, all you have to do is 'fill in the blanks' and upload your content in the same way you'd add an attachment to an email.

It's not as hard or scary as it sounds, and the best part is that the LMS industry has become so competitive now that all of them offer fabulous free training, courses and onboarding as well as incredible helpful Facebook groups for all of their users. Many have regular live Q&A's, free webinars, blogs and more with endless free advice on school set up, course creation and marketing. You'll never be alone or stuck when you're with a LMS.

The other benefit to having a LMS to host your online courses is that although YOU own your school, the software company still remain responsible for the features and have constant customer service to help you stay online! It's like having your own website without the expenses of maintenance or the responsibility of fixing software failures! Brilliant!

What Features Should Your LMS have?

Every business is different. Your products, services, audience and industry differ so much, that what functions you need your LMS to have could be remarkably different from what someone else may require.

That means that there is no set 'right' or 'wrong' as to what your LMS should have in terms of functions and features as such.

However, to be able to compete in a modern online business world, design courses with the best learner experience in mind and to make your own life easier in the meantime, here (in no particular order) are a few criteria that I would suggest putting high on your list as features that you might like your LMS to come with:

It is cloud/web based?

You want it to be cloud/web based so that your learners can access your learning from anywhere with an internet connection and without the need for complicated server set ups.

Who owns the student data?

You want to make sure that YOU own your student data and only you. You want to be able to download and view all information about your learners that they share with you, from contact information to their course progression information and that there are no restrictions to how often you may contact your own students.

Can it produce data exports?

Being able to download reports such as income reports, student progress reports and enrollment reports is highly valuable.

Does it have email and marketing integration abilities?

Building an email list is very important to any business owner. If you can automatically add all of your online course students to your own email marketing software, this will enable you to send them straight into email sequences and lists to keep in contact with them throughout their training and offer them new courses in the future.

Does it have student comments/discussion areas?

Social learning is important to increase student engagement. Students like to feel like they belong to something with other people and should be able to ask questions as they arise that other students can contribute to along with the Trainer.

Does it allow for multiple instructors to teach courses?

We are not all experts in everything, but you may have identified topics outside of your skill set that will really help your learners by adding it to your training; or even to create entire courses in conjunction with other subject matter expert instructors. This means that it would be very helpful if you can set up multiple instructor profiles and log in on your LMS so that they can amend course content, respond to student enquiries and help with course administration.

Does it allow for revenue sharing between co-instructors on courses?

If your jointly instructed courses are income generating, or you are sharing commissions on another instructors course hosted on your LMS, then it would be easier if the LMS calculated the revenue share for sales for you.

Does it have ecommerce / online payments functionality?

You don't want to be wasting your time and sanity trying to manually invoice customers for course payments, or be chasing people up for subscription payments.

Your LMS should have a simple integration for popular payment gateways such as PayPal or Stripe so that your customers can pay you upfront for your courses and automatically deduct payments from their accounts and issue receipts without your physical involvement in the transaction.

Does it allow for payments in multiple currencies?

It would be helpful for you to be able to set the currency that your courses are being charged in to the currency that matches that of the largest portion of your customer market.

Even if you are based in the UK, you might have the majority of your customers in the US and therefore need to charge in USD instead of GBP.

Can it be branded with my logos? / Can it be completely white-labelled?

It is far more professional to have a consistent look and feel of all of your products and services. From a matching colour palette, logos, images, icons, fonts and even the web URLs. Being able to highly customise your LMS site is a very valuable feature.

Does it have affiliate program functions?

The most successful online course creators have an army of affiliates behind them – people who are willing to promote their courses for them in exchange for a commission of the sale. Automating this process will make your life a million times easier. The most ideal scenario would be that your LMS allows affiliates to log in to their own dashboard area where they can generate their own affiliate links, track their own sales and income without having to contact you to conduct their sales at all.

Can you charge monthly subscriptions to users, offer bulk purchase prices, payment plans or multiple price options per course?

One method does not suit all, and you may wish to offer different payment options to your customers based on the way your course is designed and delivered, the price of it and the budgets of your customers. Having the option to charge in multiple ways will open up your opportunity for more income.

Can you create bundled course packages?

Another way to offer tailored learning options to your customers, as well as increase your chances of sales, is to have the ability to create 'bundles' of different courses for your learners. For instance you could offer 3 of your online courses as a discounted package instead of just one course; thus giving your customer a good deal and you earning more money in the exchange.

Can you schedule or 'drip feed' the release of course content to students?

Some of your courses might be better delivered in smaller parts, or with regularly released bits of content over a set period of time; this is called 'drip release'. Having an LMS that has a simple drip-release function can add

Is there a limit to the number of courses it can have?

The more courses you create, the more impact you can make and the more money you can earn. Ideally, there should not be any limit to the number of courses you create or the number of students you teach in your online LMS.

Does it have any in-platform course content creation functions?

If you are not yet ready to purchase or download your own course creation software such as screen recording equipment, it might be helpful for you to use a platform that allows you to record your voice or webcam from within the LMS course builder itself. My personal recommendation however is that you ensure that you can download these files, otherwise they will be stuck in the LMS system and you won't be able to re-use that content anywhere else for marketing, back-ups or other purposes.

Does it allow limited time free trial course access to students?

Customers love being able to 'try before they buy'. Therefore setting some (or all) of your course content to be freely available for a trial period can be a very successful way of increasing your course sales. I personally make a selection of the videos from across my courses free to encourage sign ups from those who are a little more cautious of spending their money. However, make sure that in giving away a free trial (even if it is one video), that your LMS first requires your learners to sign into your school. This way you are also using your free trials not just as a 'sales convincer', but also as a lead generating email-collector.

Does it produce course completion certificates?

This is another administrative task that you want to avoid having to add to your to-do list. Students expect completion certificates, so having an LMS that automatically generates and delivers one to them without you having to be involved in the process is a great advantage.

Does it come with get started videos / Training or on-boarding?

For those who are new to the digital realm, there is a big learning curve to go through and it can feel a bit daunting at first (but trust me, it does get easier the more you immerse yourself in it). However, to shorten the learning curve it would be very helpful to have an LMS that provides onboarding, training and support – even an online community for all of their software users, so that you can get set up and confident quickly.

Is it mobile responsive?

Today's learner's like to consume your content on the go from their handheld devices and laptops. You do not want to use an LMS that will be visually or practically compromised when viewed or accessed from a mobile device. Ensure that the LMS you are planning to use is already mobile responsive.

Does it allow for multiple assessment methods? / Can it collect and record student assessment data?

The level to which you require to collect information about student assessments, grades and evidence will depend hugely on whether you are delivering accredited or non-accredited training, who the stakeholders of your training are and much more. However, being able to collect reports about student assessments is a very helpful feature to have in your LMS – especially if you plan on providing accredited training or training to organisations of any kind.

Does it allow for any type of file upload?

To deliver quality learning experiences, your e-Learning should incorporate multiple delivery methods to suit a multitude of learning styles. Your LMS should allow for the upload and access of multiple files types such as, PDF, Word, Excel, MP3, MP4, ZIP files, images etc.

Does it have the ability for students to upload homework/documents for the trainer to mark and provide feedback?

If your training requires assessment and formal learner-teacher feedback, this is a feature that you may like to check is included as this is not always a standard LMS feature.

Does it allow for student follow up, communication, announcements and notifications?

Sending weekly update and check-in messages to your students one on one or to all enrollees as a group can really help your completion rates. You could notify them of newly released training content, homework or activities for the week or additional reading for example. Although I recommend setting up automated sequences for things like this in your email marketing system, being able to do this from directly within your LMS can be helpful for those working on a much smaller scale or the more ad-hoc notifications.

What data and analytics and tracking capabilities does it have?

You don't just want to track how students are doing once they get into your course – it's really helpful to know how they got there in the first place – better, to track who is visiting your LMS but not even buying anything so that you can alter and target your marketing activities accordingly. By integrating your LMS with tracking software like Google Analytics or social media pixels, you can find out where your referral traffic is coming from and to conduct highly targeted marketing in the future.

Does it have a functionality for live instructor led training?

Blended learning is learning that incorporates a combination of facilitated and self-directed learning components. By mixing your delivery in this way you can increase the engagement, enhance the learning experience, make distance learners feel more supported and subsequently your completion rates. Getting an LMS that enables multimedia feeds such as in-system embedding of livestreams, webinars, webcasts and podcasts for instance, is a great function for creating blended learning delivery.

Can you set open/close dates for enrollment? / Can you set expiry dates on courses?

You may be delivering training that has strict enrollment periods, term times or completion deadlines, and therefore having a feature that allows you to control the enrollment windows and expiry dates of access to your courses can be useful.

Can you create coupons and promotional codes?

There are endless reasons for creating discounts and promotional pricing for your online courses. Whether it's for a launch, special events, seasonal promos, affiliations or special customers, you'll want a super quick and simple way to create discount codes and coupons with their own expiry dates and user limits from within your LMS.

Does it allow for the school/trainers to set individual courses to public or private?

You may have some private training that is reserved especially for high end clients, or been branded to a specific client that you do not want anyone else to be able to view or access. You may have courses that you want the whole world to be able to find and buy. Therefore having the ability to be able to set each course and bundle to public, private or hidden is another helpful feature to have.

Is general admin managed by the platform?

You ideally want to automate as much of your administration as possible so that you can focus on student support and further content creation.

It's worth finding out how much of basic admin tasks your proposed LMS will manage automatically for you, such as the enrollment process, welcome emails, automatic password resetting when people have forgotten their log in details and receipt generation to name a few.

What is the pricing?
LMS platforms, although becoming more similar in their features and functions, are however still very varied in their approach to pricing. Some are free, some require one single upfront payment, some are ongoing subscriptions and some are annual payments. Pricing can range from nothing to thousands of dollars per month depending on who you choose. So carefully consider the features you want and need first, ask around those who have similar businesses and operations to you what they are using and work out what your overheads can manage as part of your decision making process.

Of course, these are not 100% of the features that LMS's have or that you might need, but they are some of the most common features out there and the most top-of-mind ones to be aware of as a consideration in your selection.

Hopefully this section has provided some insight for you to go in a little more informed.

Which LMS Do I Use?

There are quite literally hundreds of popular LMS's out there, but my personal favorite at the time of writing this books is Thinkific and I've chosen this for me for a number of reasons that suit my personal situation, preferences and business needs.

Before going with my suggestion however, I strongly suggest that you pick a handful and sign up to the free trials of them all (they all have a free trial option).

In terms of features, most of the LMS platforms out there are pretty similar these days. There's so much competition out there now that when one gets a sexy new feature the rest of them are pretty quick to follow up and get the same, too.

They all have slightly different user interfaces, slightly different user communities and so it is best that you try for yourself rather than taking other people's suggestions – what works for one person may not work for you.

Therefore the choice really comes down to your own personal 'feeling' of the platform, rather than whether there is one that's 'the best' anymore.

If you want to see just how simple it is to create and sell your own online courses, go to YouTube and search for 'Sarah Cordiner Thinkific' and you'll find a list of demo videos I've created on how to set your own school up. I also have a free webinar on how to create your own online school on Thinkific here: www.sarahcordiner.com/thinkificdemo

Online Course Website Software & Plugins

The third major way of hosting and selling your own online courses is with website plugins or website software.

These 'plugins' and 'software' are a little like 'apps' that you upload to your website and allow you to upload your courses and have very similar features to a LMS – but all on your own fully owned digital land.

This is the ultimate ownership and is the equivalent of buying a house outright. You make the investment (some plugins and software are subscription payments, some you buy outright) and you are completely on your own.

Although this brings many benefits, such as complete design freedom, sometimes more advanced features that you could get a developer to code up for you and the removed risk of a third party platform shutting down; the reason why I personally, have chosen to host all of my courses on a LMS, a piece of software outside of my website, is because websites can crash.

Websites require maintenance, websites require you to be able to respond very quickly if things go wrong. And when things go wrong on websites, it can be very very expensive and time consuming to get it fixed.

True story: Just before Christmas 2016 I'd just conducted a massive Christmas marketing campaign and on the big day of the Christmas sale my website crashed. It died, and it was down for FOUR DAYS during what was supposed to be my biggest promotional activity of the year. Luckily, because my online school is hosted off of my website, it didn't affect my sales, it didn't affect my business and it didn't affect my students who were using the Christmas period as a time to do some self-development.

What I do have on my website is a page called 'Courses' that auto redirects to my online school.

This way the URL I give out for my LMS is www.sarahcordiner.com/courses.

This is easy to remember, good for branding, but also is important for more operational reasons too.

It is important that all of your marketing material goes via your website primarily so that you are promoting YOUR brand, not the brand of the LMS provider! But also because if the LMS provider ever did disappear, or I wanted to switch to another one later on, then none of my marketing that's out there in the world (and I have a lot of it) would have to change. I simply would only have to change the auto redirect on my website, not the hundreds of thousands of links that I have on thousands of bits of content I've created.

Another reason for this is that a good website will have tracking pixels on it – a way to collect the data of people who visit your website so that you can directly send advertising to them that may be relevant in the future. By directing people through your site, you are able to get the real picture of your site popularity and customer analytics.

With plugins comes the ultimate power and control, but it also comes with risk and responsibility. This option is best reserved for those with some tech savvy or a good web developer that they can afford to keep close all of the time.

Which Platform Should You Use?

I believe you should be using all of them.

All of them have very different pros and cons, all of them are used in different stages of your business funnel, and therefore all of them should be seen as different elements of your business delivery system and your marketing system, as well.

You need to have the marketplaces to bring in paying students in volume who may be interested in migrating to your primary platform.

You need to have the LMS or the plugins in order to be able to then deliver that product under your own roof, under your own control and under your own banner.

In summary, make sure that in your marketing you are sending people to your website; that your website has a 'courses' tab that auto redirects people to your school, and outside of that you're using online course marketplaces as a way to gain yourself paid exposure and new leads to direct to your own LMS. Note that you are always directing prospects from the marketplaces to your own platform. Never direct people from your own platform to a marketplace – that would be equivalent to doing somebody else's marketing for them.

Use your website as a way to get leads into your own LMS by publishing searchable content from it such as blogs and videos, which all upsell and promote your courses.

CHAPTER 7

HOW ALL OF THE PARTS OF YOUR ONLINE EDU-BUSINESS FIT TOGETHER

Building an online business for the first time is challenging!

I see many new online entrepreneurs giving themselves a real hard time about it all - thinking that they have to know it ALL right away.

There is a lot to take in and it does take a long time to learn - especially if technology is all brand new to you.

You must remember that absolutely nobody falls out of the womb knowing how to work all of this stuff out - you quite simply just have to roll your sleeves up, get stuck in, have a play about and learn it.

Once you do, it's incredibly satisfying and actually very fun.

It has taken me a few years to really wrap my head around the world of online business, and I believe a lot of my success is down to the fact that I love learning as much as I love teaching. Because when you live online, you live in a world that never stops changing. Just as you finally master something, 10 more new things pop up that you can play with too!

So the trick here is to know that there is no single correct way of running your online business. There are endless combinations of bringing all of your online components together, and not one of them is right or wrong.

The more you learn and the more confident you get, the more intricate you can make your online funnels, systems, apps, integrations and processes.

But for now, here is a much bigger picture of how all of your online education business can fit together from a birds eye view.

This video is to show you how your website, online school, online course marketplaces, lead magnets, email lists and email marketing all combine together to form the backbone of a successful online business.

"How do I connect all of my stuff together when I run an online business"? I hear you scream.

We've got websites, we've got online schools, we've got email lists, we've got email marketing, we've got payment platforms, this stuff just gets very overwhelming when you're first starting out.

There is a lot to think about, and there's all kinds of advice out there telling you what to do.

So the first thing I'm going to say is that there is no single one way of doing any of this stuff. There are multiple combinations, there are a billion different types of platforms out there.

Do go and research them all, do the free trials of them all, find the ones that work best for you.

I will now share with you some of the methods that I use to keep my online business ticking along effectively, including the main components that run it all and some of my most important tools and software. My aim is that sharing this will help you understand the bigger picture and how the major pieces of a successful online business fit together.

Watch The Tutorial Video

If you prefer to watch a training video on this instead of reading, you can watch a free 30 minute tutorial from me here: https://sarahcordiner. com/how-all-of-the-parts-of-your-online-business-fit-together/

Your Website

When you're running an online business, first think about what are the products and services that you actually have.

Since this book is tailored for Edupreneurs, I'm going to assume that you have some kind of educational or information type products to sell, particularly online courses or books.

If you're selling online courses, your online school (LMS) is central to your online business.

However, all of your marketing should be focussed on sending all of your traffic to your website, NOT your LMS.

Ensure that your website includes at minimum:

- a blog (that you preferably publish regularly)
- details about all of your products and services
- hosts all of the landing pages for your products and services
- has a quote request form
- has a page specifically for your online courses
- has a specific page for your books and eBooks
- showcases everything that you have to offer your customers
- has an 'about you' page which includes your keynote presentations
- has contact details
- online calendar booking
- social media share buttons
- has tracking pixels for retargeting later
- has a google analytics account

Protect Your Assets and Efforts

Don't make all of your marketing point directly to our online school.

Why?

You need to make sure that you are building a safe and sustainable online business that allows you to capture 100% of our customer data and ownership.

If you're using an external piece of software, marketplace or platform to host your online courses and sending all of our traffic to that third party software, what happens if that software disappears, crashes or the business goes under? Who gets to collect the pixel data of the platform visitors and who owns the customer?

Don't work hard and spend your marketing money to grow somebody else's brand for them.

Make sure everyone always gets sent to your website first – then your website can redirect them to your online courses wherever they are hosted.

If your marketing is sending your customers directly to an external platform, and that external platform shuts down for any reason; then you will have all of your marketing sending people to a now redundant school, instead of to a website that you own and can create redirects from.

I send everyone to my own website, and from my website then redirect people to the courses and products they want to purchase. That way, I could change my hosting platforms or methods anytime I wanted and I'd never have to change all of my marketing that's gone out to the world (which would be the links on hundreds of YouTube videos, blogs, articles, social media posts and podcasts); I'd only have to change the redirect on my website.

Even if you OWN the third party software, best practice is to always ensure that every piece of marketing you have going out to the world, always sends people back to your website, NOT to the third party LMS.

Look at my website www.sarahcordiner.com. If you click on my 'Courses' tab, it'll first show my customers all of my course offerings on my website. Then, if my customers sign up to any courses, it will take them to my online school.

ALL of my marketing for my online courses tells my customers to go to www.sarahcordiner.com/courses which simply redirects them to my external LMS. If for any reason I changed LMS providers, I simply change the redirect and none of my marketing is affected.

Promote Your Other Products and Services

Another reason why you should send people to your own website instead of someone else's third party platform is so that you can promote and offer your other products and services.

How many times have you gone to the store to buy a very specific item, and then come out with bags full of items that you had no intention of buying whatsoever? I know I have many times!

People need to know and see what you have on offer in order to be able to buy it.

You may have keynote talks that you offer, books and eBooks, multiple online courses, services, consulting and more. If you are sending people to a platform away from your website, then they won't have the opportunity to window shop past all of the other offerings you may have.

I have designed my website in a way that ensures every single page shows what I have on offer to make it as easy as possible for people to buy from me.

Simply create page templates so that every time you post a new blog post, all of your sales widgets and offers are automatically embedded into the page; minimising your effort and maximising your conversions. If you take a look at any of my blog posts (www.sarahcordiner.com/blog) you will see how on every page there are free challenges that readers can take, online course discounts or freebies, lists of upcoming events and services in the menu bars and after the articles. I'd highly recommend that you speak to your web developer and get similar items in place.

After all, if your website is not growing your email list and making you money, it's not working properly!

Collect Customer Data For Retargeting & Analytics

Have you ever gone onto Google and searched for flight prices to your favourite holiday destination, and then been followed everywhere by discount flight and accommodation prices to that destination on social media adverts?

This is 'pixels' at work.

If you visit a website that has tracking pixels on it, it captures your devices IP address (legally) and the owner of that website can then serve very specific adverts to that IP address across the internet pages that you visit based on what you were searching for or looking at. This is called 'retargeting' in the industry.

You can do the same to your website visitors too, which is why you want people to go to your site, not someone else's. Even though you don't get 'actual' contact details, you still gather data that's just as powerful as an email list in many ways.

With tracking pixels, you now have the ability to be able to retarget marketing and advertising to very specific people who have taken very specific actions on your website; such as read a specific blog post, bought a specific product, viewed a certain page and clicked on a certain link. Simply ask your web developer if they can add your Facebook tracking pixel to your website for you and it will immediately start collecting this data ready for you to 'target' your adverts at if you do any paid advertising on Facebook. Note that Facebook is not the only site that can give you tracking pixels.

Collect Email Addresses To Grow Your List

Your email list is considered an asset in the valuation of your business. Whether you're selling your business or not, the message here is that your list means money.

Every person on your email list is an existing or potential customer (known as leads), and therefore needs to be counted as a highly valuable and very important asset.

The more of the right people you have on your email list, the more potential income you have.

So the objective is to identify who your ideal customer is, and then conduct various activities over time to grow the number of those identified types of people who's contact details you have – and actually contact them.

Make it easy for people to 'join your contact list', by having sign up boxes on your website. This doesn't to be the old fashioned 'sign up to our newsletter' pop up, but could be a free gift that you offer in exchange for their email address (you can read more about this in the next section).

Either way, getting people on your email list should always be a high priority so that you can build a relationship with them and keep them engaged with you and your business.

Lead Magnets

Now that we've talked about leads, let's now master the concept of lead magnets.

For those who don't know what lead magnets are, they are something that you offer to your prospective customer in exchange for their email address.

Lead magnets are the proverbial carrot on a stick to attract your target customers through your digital door.

However, the 'something' that you offer obviously has to be tasty, exciting, and useful to the people who are looking at it in order for them to want to exchange their email address for it – and it has to be specifically selected and designed to attract only your perfect customer.

In these days, people hate giving their email address away because they're pretty certain that they're going to get bombarded with sales emails and stuff like that. So you've got to make sure that the thing you're offering is valuable enough for people to go, yeah, it's going to be worth getting a bit of junk mail for this, because that's how people are thinking. So, lead magnets, this could be anything.

This could be a taster version of your online course, it could be the recording of a useful webinar, it could be an eBook, it could be a physical book, it could be a free consultation session. There's all sorts of things that you could use as a free gift in exchange for that email address because once you have that email address, obviously you can then take whatever that free information product or gift was that's the same topic as your online course, you know that if they've downloaded that free thing, they are clearly interested in that topic, they're clearly interested in finding out information about that thing, and therefore it's quite likely that after a taster of you that was free that they might then want to pay a little bit of money to then take some of your paid products or services.

So, what I do is I take either a free recording of a free webinar, or I use a taster version of my course, just small sample, enough to give people value, enough to get them started on something, to show them that I do have the information that I promise. This is your opportunity to show people that you're not just making up the fact that you know what you're talking about. It's an opportunity for you to demonstrate that you actually know your stuff, it's an opportunity for you to demonstrate and prove that you are who you say you are, that you have the expertise that you're offering to charge people money to give them.

So, make your lead magnet, if you can, something that's got video in it so that they can have that experience of you. This is where the real trust comes in, this is where people no longer have any doubts about you because they've seen for themselves that you know what you're saying.

48 Lead Magnet Ideas

There is no end to what you could offer to people in exchange for their contact details – be creative and think very hard about what they need, and make sure that whatever it is is highly relevant to your edu-products and services.

There is no point offering a healthy eating meal plan if your online course is about web design – you'll be attracting completely the wrong type of people!

The whole point of a lead magnet is to attract the perfect customer to you and your business and to give them something that they value before trying to sell to them.

Below are 48 random lead magnet ideas to help inspire you.

Have a read through and think about which ones could work for you and be most attractive to your perfect audience.

1. Cheatsheet
2. A list of the best books for 'target client'
3. Free Report
4. Top online apps, web tools for 'target client'
5. State of your industry predictions
6. Free time saver (template, checklist, flow charts, cheat sheets) any kind of short cut that your client will find useful
7. Contact lists that target client will want
8. A list of the most helpful websites for 'target client'
9. Toolkit
10. Best Facebook groups, forums, online communities for 'target client'
11. Checklist
12. Resource List
13. Processes or procedures
14. Guides
15. Video(s)
16. Quizzes
17. Mind Map
18. MP3 / Audio recordings
19. Free gift voucher or credit voucher
20. Free 'test drive'
21. Free sample
22. Free trial
23. Free quote
24. Free review / assessment
25. Free advice
26. Free consultation
27. Recipes
28. Process Flow Diagram
29. Scripts
30. Timetables / Schedules

31. Event Recordings
32. Online Course
33. Free webinar
34. Infographic
35. Giveaway packages that include other people's products/services
36. Templates
37. Blueprints
38. Audio Book
39. Podcast
40. Slideshare / Powerpoint
41. Answers to 10 FAQs that your clients ask
42. Transcripts (of courses, interviews etc)
43. Actions plans
44. Offer a 'bundle' of the best stuff for a discount if they buy it right there and then
45. Books
46. eBooks
47. 10 fixes to common problems your audience have
48. Free Branded Materials

Delivering Your Lead Magnets

How you get your 'thing' to your audience will obviously depend on what you are giving to them, but my advice would be to make it simple to start with. Just offer something digital so that you don't have to worry about having any physical stock or manage the complexities of shipping.

There are a number of ways to deliver lead magnets and there really isn't a 'right' or 'wrong' way of doing it.

As long as people can get what they gave their email address for, you're all good.

For those who plan to have lots of lead magnets or higher end offerings and who have a budget, you can buy specialised software that is solely designed to create high converting lead pages and auto deliver the digital 'thing' that you promised in complete automation.

But there are also ways to do this completely for free; AND to then create a tailored experience for that collected 'lead' (customer) that will nurture them into becoming a loyal fan and buyer.

Here is just one of the endless ways that you can deliver a lead magnet.

This particular method is done using a combination of:

- Google Drive (where the lead magnet is stored – but can also be stored directly on your website)
- Active Campaign (the email marketing software that delivers it to them and keeps their email address for future marketing),
- and my website (to build the landing page).

My website has a super simple 'drag and drop' building feature installed on it so that I can create really professional looking pages in minutes by just dragging and dropping the elements I want onto my page.

I will explain this second method as this will give you lots of different tips and information that will serve you in more than just delivering a lead magnet! Also, this is a method that can be done on zero budget.

Before I delve in, I will again reiterate that this is only one of many ways that you can deliver a lead magnet, I'm not claiming that this is the 'best' or 'right' way of doing it, as all businesses are different and need different tools and methods for their unique operations; however this is certainly a method that works.

Store your Lead Magnet Somewhere 'Online'

Google Drive is part of the Google platform (also known as GSuite).

As a quick 'by the way', Google Docs, Google Sheets, Google Slides (which are only some of the many GSuite goodies), are basically free versions of Microsoft Word, Microsoft Excel, Microsoft PowerPoint, but they are on the cloud. So no matter what device you're using you have access to all of your documents, you're never going to lose documentation, you never have multiple versions of anything, you can even collaborate with your team, freelancers, or clients working on those documents live.

However, part of the extensive Google platform is something called Google Drive, which put simply is an online document storage facility.

If had a free eBook (or any other form of document or digital file) that I wanted to deliver as a lead magnet, all I have to do is upload it to my Google Drive first. (Please note that you can also upload files directly to your website 'media files' area too, but not everyone reading this will have a website. However everyone reading this can easily make a Google Drive for free within minutes – hence I'm using this example).

When you upload something to a Google Drive it gives that file a URL, and you can change the permissions to that particular file, to 'only you can view it' (so it's private), or you can specifically only invite certain people by putting their email address into the permission area; or you can switch it to 'only people with a link can view this file' or you can switch it to 'public' so that anyone on the internet could find this document using the keywords that you've made in the title.

Set your file to 'public' and ensure the edit permission is 'can view only' (you don't want them being able to *edit* your version).

Like this, you could quite simply just give people the link, and they will be able to access that file and make their own copy of it.

Collect Your Customer's Email Address

In this particular instance for delivering a lead magnet, you will then want to have an email marketing system to collect the email addresses and auto-deliver the lead magnet by email to your customer.

I use Active Campaign for this as it has many more helpful features than just sending emails.

In Active Campaign, create a 'form'.

The form is where people will enter in their name, their email address and any other information fields you'd like to add, and the submission of that form is what will trigger the email to be sent to the customer which contains your lead magnet.

Keep the form as short as possible – the more people have to type in, the less likely they will be to submit it. People don't like sharing their personal information so you'll lose prospects if you ask for more information than is required. First name and email address is enough to deliver a lead magnet.

Send the Lead Magnet

Once you have created the form that your prospects will fill in to get their lead magnet, you then need to create an auto-response email to deliver it to them.

This is known in the online marketing world as an 'email automation', which is basically a sequence of emails that sends to a prospect following a certain 'trigger'.

In this instance, the 'trigger' is the form being submitted.

In Active Campaign, you would now go to 'Automations', create a new automation and select the 'trigger' (what starts the sequence) as 'when someone submits X form'.

Your 'sequence' of emails could simply be one single email which includes the link to your eBook.

If you'd like some full training on how to set up email automations using Active Campaign, I have lots of training videos in the Edupreneur Academy (www.sarahcordiner.com/academy), and on my YouTube channel (www.sarahcordiner.com/youtube).

CHAPTER 8

BECOME AN INDUSTRY LEADER

It doesn't stop here.

Now you have made a plan about how you will start to commercialise your expertise by creating education based products and services, the next level is to decide how you will begin to get your expertise to precede you and bring in a constant stream of business on brand new levels as an industry leader.

You may have seen those well-known 'experts' in your industry and wondered how they got themselves there.

How did they get all of those followers?

How did they win those awards?

How do they always get on the stages, in the magazines and interviewed on podcasts?

Let me let you into a little secret.

It's because they voted themselves in to start with.

Nobody is going to build your throne for you. You have to build it yourself.

I nominate MYSELF for awards, or ASK my clients if they will nominate me.

I don't wait for magazines to ask me if I'll be a contributor, I identify magazines that I want to write for and send my articles to them with a request for it to be published.

I contact podcasters and present them with a suggested topic for their show and offer to share that topic expertise to their listeners; I don't wait to be invited to speak at conferences, I trawl the international conference directories for the best events in my industry and send them a list of topics I can speak about.

None of these successes happen by accident. If you want it, you have to go and get it yourself and you have to start today.

Courses Are The New Business Card

Create an online course and make it your 'business card'.

Everywhere you go, everything you do, every time you write, present or get interviewed in front of a brand new audience, give an online course away.

This will get you new connections and enable people to 'experience' you – they are unlikely to forget the face of a helpful online course, whereas a small rectangular piece of card is likely to end up in their trash.

A business card is just some contact information, with no compelling reason to ever use.

Whereas an online course ensures that a funnel is entered, an experience is had, a memory is made, a result is obtained and a customer is gained – all whilst proving to that person that you are the 'real deal'. A business card can't ever do that, no matter how enthusiastically it is handed over.

Work Together

Think about how you can leverage your exposure by strategically working with others.

Who or what does your customer use or work with before or after you? What do they need to have, do or know before or after you?

Work with those product or service providers and make them a proposal for collaboration of some kind.

Please make sure you approach them with an outlined idea or clearly articulated suggestion that explicitly outlines what they get and what you get as a result of the specified arrangement. There is nothing that will send you to the spam folder quicker than sending a completely vague email that says *'Hey! I wondered if we could have a quick chat or meet up to come up with some ideas for collaboration?!'*. If somebody looks like they can't be bothered to even come up with an idea, yet wants your whole audience from you, you're probably going to say no, right?

Give influencers a magnetic and compelling reason to want to pick up the phone and give you their time. Busy people do not have the time or inclination to chat about nothing.

Example of how I have partnered with others:
As an example, I worked out that after people have learned how to create an online course, they then need somewhere to host it. I also knew from being in the industry that many people who already had a platform, hadn't created a course yet. So I found an online course software company who I respected and we teamed up in a way that we both would benefit. I would gift every one of their paid members access to my *'How To Create Profitable* Courses' online course for FREE. That made their package look even more attractive to their customers, and although I lost a course sale, I gained a new highly targeted customer I'd not otherwise have gained - without spending any money in marketing.

I had one customer who was a divorce attorney and she was selling her time for money by the hour. I asked her who else her customers would need to see before or after her, and we came up with a list of people such as lawyers, estate agents and even massage therapists and psychotherapists! I encouraged her to contact the big list of people we came up with and she secured tens of thousands of dollars in referral fees and discount vouchers for her users so that she could generate strategic partnerships for cross-directional referrals, alternative income streams and ways to increase her package pricing.

Activity: Your Partners

Who could you team up with?

Make a list of at least 20 people, companies, products and services that your perfect customer might use or need before or after you.

Remember that the partner doesn't necessarily have to have anything directly to do with your industry at all.

Re-Purpose Your Expertise

An online course is an excellent first step product.

The way that it needs to be organised and designed, as well as the online structural set up it requires, means that you have everything you need to continue reproducing and selling more content thereafter.

The key is to remember that everyone likes to consume information in different ways, so you don't have to work 10 times harder to get 10 times the reach. You simply have to take one single video from your course and share it in ways where more people can find it.

The more you can repurpose your content into every different medium possible, the more your global student base will grow

Start thinking about how your course could later turn into your own:

Podcast

For anyone wanting to become an authority in their industry, a podcast is such a great method to consider using.

I had been meaning to start the Course Creators Podcast for such a long time, but life always took over.

I met a lot of successful people in 2016 and asked them what contributed to their success – and for many of them, their podcasts were top of the list. I knew I HAD to get my podcast out by 2017.

I read every blog article I could find on 'How To Create a Podcast' and followed every step they offered.

Within a few days I was up and running, and couldn't believe how much simpler it was than I'd imagined.

I was ecstatic to have implemented yet another way of sharing my content with the world – but then it got unexpectedly better......

Within the FIRST DAY of going live, I made $588 in online course sales WITHOUT ADVERTISING. At that point I hadn't even emailed it out to my email community – I just went live. That's it.

The thing that is most surprising about this, is that at this stage I wasn't even on an audio directory. I wasn't yet on iTunes, or Stitcher or any of the other listed sites. The ONLY thing I did was put it on YouTube and share it on my Facebook – with people who ALREADY knew me, knew my content and knew about my online courses!!! This is why it was such a surprise as I didn't expect to make sales from people who already knew I had the course for sale.

What it showed me, was that it doesn't matter how many times you share your content – as long as you are sharing it in as many different forms as you possibly can. Some people like to watch videos, some livestreams, some like to read and others like to listen. Also, people are familiar with podcasts and so trust them more than they'd trust an email or an ad.

Have you thought about creating your own podcast next year? I'm so glad I did

Blogs and Articles

Every online course is essentially a collection of tips, advice and strategies for something.

Pull out every single tip and strategy from your online course and write a short blog post about each one.

If you have already filmed your online course, then you'll be pleased to know that you have already done most of the hard work. Simply transcribe all of your online course videos and turn them into blog posts! I use Rev.com to transcribe all of my videos. The great thing about this, is that not only do you get the text file, you also get the closed caption files too – all for $1 per minute of video.

Not only will your own website be more discoverable in search engine results due to the keyword content and data in your blogs; but you can also repurpose those blogs as articles and send them to industry relevant magazines. Getting an article related to your online course into a popular online magazine could get your course in front of hundreds of thousands of highly targeted readers.

Blogging continues to have a huge return on investment for me and will always remain top of my marketing list.

Publish Books

Another great way to repurpose your online course into other income generating educational content, is to transcribe every video of your course and turn it into a print book or eBook.

Books are a fantastic way to reach your audience at a global level. Simply upload your book on to the Amazon platform and you'll immediately have your content open to over 63 million people.

The added benefit of this is that your book and your courses then begin to promote one another. I add a free course into my books and promote that as a bonus on the cover. This encourages readers to buy the book. I also encourage my online course students to buy the books.

It's not as difficult as you might think now that self-publishing has become so accessible to the world. If you want to learn how to become a self-published author, I have an online course on the exact writing, publishing and printing process in my Edupreneur Academy, called *'How To Write and Self-Publish Your Own Print Book and eBook':* (www.sarahcordiner. com/academy)

Keynote Speech

Public speaking is a highly lucrative profession and grows your brand rapidly.

Imagine being invited to an event that thousands of people have paid to attend, and they are all your perfect audience?

You're on the stage as an expert and being there automatically makes you the audiences' guru.

Take your online course and turn it into a 30min, 60min and 90min presentation.

Wow them with some really juicy bits of your expertise and then either give your course away for free at the end so that you get them all as leads – OR sell your course from the stage to make some more income.

Magazine Column

I started repurposing my video content into articles and sending them to magazines so frequently, that I landed myself a few regular columns in magazines and have subsequently reached hundreds of thousands of people through other people's platforms,. When my name is typed into Google, results come up from all kinds of sites hosting my content – this proves my credibility to customers and wins me more business.

I later decided to create my own magazine and published 'Edupreneur Magazine' in early 2017. I never imagined that what would start as some simple tip videos, would later turn into my running my own publication.

All of this is possible when you commit and consistently execute.

YouTube Channel

YouTube has over 1 billion users. You'd be crazy not to tap into that global platform.

Add a selection of the videos from your online course to YouTube. You can now schedule the publication of your YouTube videos so that they drip publish over a period of time and maximise your exposure. Create a discount coupon to your course and add it to the YouTube video description to entice the global viewers into your courses.

Make sure you add a really detailed description to your YouTube video and give it a title that people are likely to be typing into Google or YouTube, so that your video comes up as the number 1 search result!

Be Omnipresent

Finally, be present and omnipresent online.

People spend their lives attached to their mobile devices these days and they are more likely to buy who and what appears in front of them, rather than go looking for things to spend their money and time on.

If you are not in front of them, then you don't exist to them.

So join the Facebook groups they are in, engage in conversation, be helpful, answer questions, offer to help, don't always go for the sale, make friends, share people's stuff, share your own stuff and make the effort to have content and your face on every platform that your audience are on.

The second you stop sharing, is the second you stop selling.

Different mediums will work better for you depending on your audience and your topic; but you've got to start to find out which it is.

Remember that every piece of content you create is going to serve you later, buy you more time later and bring you more customers through search results later.

A little investment right now, will have a future you sending a message of thanks right back.

Start Right Now

Please don't 'wait' for anything to start commercialising your expertise.

Today is the perfect time to start.

Today is the only opportunity you can count on for taking the first tiny step.

You've been practicing for this your entire life so please do your entire life some credit by starting to share what you know now.

It can be a lead magnet, it could be a blog post to start showing your expertise and collecting a readership, or it could be creating your first online course.

Pick ONE goal, ONE tiny task that you can start today.

My intention for this book was to inspire you to take some action, to provide a bigger picture for where your edupreneurial journey could go in the longer term, and to help you establish some direction and actionable tasks to get moving.

Activity: Time To Hit The Road

1. What is your number 1 goal for your life?
2. What are the top 3 tasks that you need to do in order to make that goal come to life?
3. Write a 'declaration' of what you will achieve in the next 12 months
4. Write the top 5 things that you got from this book that you will not allow yourself to forget in order to keep progressing
5. Share your declaration and top 5 things to remember from this book in my Facebook group 'Entrepreneur to Edupreneur – Course Creators' so that you are accountable and inspire others.

Resources

Free Course: Create Your First Online Course Outline

All great products, start with a great plan.

Although this is not always the most fun part of getting out to the world, a good course outline is critical for creating a course that will make you shine and give your learners a great learning experience.

I have a **FREE 5 day challenge** that take you through the step by step process of getting your online course completely mapped out by the 6th day: www.sarahcordiner.com/courseplanchallenge

Free Edupreneur's Community

My Facebook group 'Entrepreneur to Edupreneur' is a place that anyone can join to ask questions and hang out with people from all around the world on the same journey.

The Edupreneur Academy

I have packed well over 40 online courses and books into the Edupreneur Academy that are all designed especially for the Edupreneur. From course creation, book publishing, online marketing, presenting, business development and much more, there are always more courses and books being added to the private members area.

The Edupreneur Academy is a paid monthly membership (at the time of publishing this edition of this book it was $47 per month and the first 30 days are FREE - but may have gone up since than). The monthly fee gives you unlimited access to all resources and courses inside the academy members area.

You can check out what the members get and start your 30 day FREE TRIAL in the Edupreneur Academy here: www.sarahcordiner.com/academy

Other Books By Sarah Cordiner

All of the following titles are available for purchase on Amazon: www.sarahcordiner.com/books

- The Theory And Principles Of Creating Effective Training Courses: *What To Do Before Creating Your Course*
- Awaken Your Course Creation Mojo: *Beat Procrastination And Fire Up Your Course Creation Motivation*
- Maximising Staff Training on a Minimum Budget
- How To Build a Facebook Community and Sell More Online Courses

Contact Sarah:

Website: www.sarahcordiner.com

Youtube: https://www.sarahcordiner.com/youtube

LinkedIn: https://www.linkedin.com/in/sarahcordiner

Twitter: https://twitter.com/CordinerSarah

Entrepreneur to EDUpreneur Facebook Group: https://www.facebook.com/groups/entrepreneur2edupreneur/

Facebook: https://www.facebook.com/cordinersarah

Please leave a review!

I would love your feedback about this book.

As an author, reviews are extremely important for our business. It would mean a great deal to me if you might be able to leave a review on Amazon.

Simply go to www.sarahcordiner.com/books and you will be taken to the Amazon link.

Thank you in advance.

23555701R00099

Printed in Poland
by Amazon Fulfillment
Poland Sp. z o.o., Wrocław